NĀ KAONA

HAWAIIAN METAPHORICAL POETRY

NĀ KAONA

HAWAIIAN METAPHORICAL POETRY

WAYNE MONIZ AND FRIENDS

Punawai Press
1812 Nani St.
Wailuku, Maui
Hawai`i 96793

Distributed in America and Worldwide by
Pūnāwai Press, Amazon Books, and Kindle.
For more about the book and author,
search online for the title and/or Wayne Moniz.

Moniz, Wayne
Nā Kaona: Hawaiian Metaphorical Poetry. Also
kaona by guest writers, other different poetic
genre and song lyrics by Wayne Moniz, Includes
glossary of Hawaiian words and a poetic drama.
Wayne Moniz, Wailuku, Maui, Hawai`i:
Punawai Press, © 2022

ISBN: 9798363771613

Includes poetry by other guest writers and
definitions of Hawaiian words.
1. Hawai`i *Kaona* - Poetry. 2. Hawaiian
Metaphorical Poetry. 3. Hidden meaning poetry.
4. Nature poetry. 5. Maui poetry. Play about `Īao
Valley, Maui, Hawai`i.

INTRODUCTION
BY THE AUTHOR

The Hawaiian word for "hidden meaning" is *kaona*. Mary Pukui, the great Hawai`i historian and culturalist (*Songs (Mele) of Old Ka`u,* 1949: 247-251), said, "There are two meanings to the *mele* : the literal and the *kaona* or inner meaning. The literal is like the body, and the inner meaning is like the spirit of the poem."

Vagueness, lack of sexual gender, verbs without subjects or objects and subjects without verbs are often part of the makeup of such *mele.* However, the focus is on elements in nature that represent people, places, things and events in the Rites of Life, e.g. birth, death, marriage, love, achievements, people that we admire or, merely, friendships.

The *kaona* is simply what most students learn in their literature classes as the extended metaphor that incorporates the other forms of figurative language - simile, personification, and symbolism.

The Hawaiians had no printed grammar until the missionaries arrived and converted their oral language into a written one as well. So in pre-contact times when an occasion arose to express oneself, the composer created it by inspiration (*mana`o ulu wale*) and memorized it. He or she then recited it orally to the individual (e.g. a *mele* for my mother on her birthday) or to a related group of people (a poem to the siblings of a deceased person). It was a message sometimes discernible only to the recipient of the *mele.*

"*Kaona*", according to Kamehameha Schools' *Haku Mele* Project, "showcases the composer's level of skill, the knowledge of his/her audience, the complexity of composition, an indicator of intelligence, and the ability to connect the present to the past." It heavily utilizes the five senses. It proudly displays the sophistication of our early Hawaiian ancestors. For a more extensive examination of *kaona*, check out Brandy Nālani McDougall's book, *Finding Meaning: Kaona and Contemporary Hawaiian Literature.*

To stimulate his/her writing, the poet chooses the person or subject of the poem and recalls an element of nature related to them and that has the same, though not so apparent, qualities. The more common elements (though not limited to these) are birds, fish and sea creatures, flowers, plants, trees, mountains, rains and mists, ocean, rivers, and winds. All these are referred to specifically - e.g birds: the *nēnē*, fish: *akule*, flowers: *loke lani,* plants: *`uki `uki* berry, trees: *hala*, mountains: *Haleakalā*, rains: *Wa`ahila*, mists: *noenoe,* ocean: *Kahana* Bay: rivers: Wailuku, winds: *A`e* (tradewind).

A waterfall, for example, should also be

specific like the *kaona, Honokohau*. That *kaona*, that appears in this book, is the name of the tallest waterfall in the West Maui Mountains. The waterfall has the same, though indiscernible, qualities of the person or subject for whom the poem was composed.

The Hawaiian form of poetry is similar to the works of the American school of Transcendentalism that includes the great poetic giants: Emerson, Thoreau, Whitman and Dickinson.

This book, that includes poems I've collected from over thirty years, is separated in categories. The First Section is *kaona* dedicated to the memory of the passing of family and friends (Celebration of Life). Section Two is for birthdays. Section Three presents *kaona* from other poets. Section Four includes examples of other forms of poetry. Section Five features Wayne's song lyrics. Section Six is a BONUS - an unpublished Poetic Drama about the life of ʻĪao Valley.

To help you with the Hawaiian language, I've provided vocabulary (*Nā Hua ʻŌlelo*) on the opposite left page of each *kaona*. *Kaona* that run over one page are completed on the left page prior to the *nā hua ʻōlelo* translations.

The general readership may miss the full scope of these personally composed gifts to another but nonetheless should appreciate the vivid imagery of nature.

I hope you enjoy *Nā Kaona*.

"The goal of life
Is to make your heartbeat
match the beat of the Universe,
To match your nature
with Nature."

Joseph Campbell

TABLE OF CONTENTS

☆

Page 15. CELEBRATIONS OF LIFE - by Wayne Moniz

Page 17.   Ka Roselani

Page 19.   Ka Panini o Ka Punahou

Page 21.   Ka `Awapuhi Ke`o Ke`o o Kaleponi

Page 23.   Ka Manakō

Page 25.   Ka Pukanawila

Page 27.   Ka Pua Keli

Page 29-30.   Ka Puakenikeni

Page 31.   Ka Lehua Kula o Hawai`i Nui

Page 33.   Ka Mahina Loke

Page 35.   Ka Lauhihi

Page 37-38.   Ka Ua Ho`opala `Ōhi`a

Page 39.   Ka Pa`a Male Paina

Page 41.   Ka Lei o No`e

Page 43.   Ka Pua Helohelo

Page 45-46.   Ka `Awapuhi `Ula`ula o `Īao

Page 47-48.   Ka Lei Ponimō`ī `Ula Kālua
Page 49-50.   Ka `Ukulele
Page 51.   Ke Koholā
Page 53.   Ka Ulua
Page 55.   Ka `Ula`ula
Page 57.   Ka Moi
Page 59.   Ke Kōlea
Page 61-62.   Ka Hua Waina
Page 63-64.   Ke Kō o Pu`ukoli`i
Page 65.   Ke Kalo
Page 67.   Ka Hōkū Welowelo
Page 69.   Ke Koa
Page 71-72.   Ka Ua Ke`oke`o o Hāna
Page 73.   Lehua Mau Loa
Page 75-76.   Ke Kanaka Lu`u i Ka
              Hohonu Pōhaku
Page 77-78.   Ka La`au `Ula`ula o
              Kaleponi
Page 79-80.   Nā Moku lua

Page 81. BIRTHDAYS
by Wayne Moniz

Page 83. Ke Ao `Ākala Mo`oni

Page 85. He Lei Kamali`i

Page 87. Kaulana `Oe, E Ka Pua Pīkake

Page 89-90. Ka Pua Melia o Maleka
　　　　　　Kamika

Page 91-92. Dedications

☆

Page 93. KAONA BY FRIENDS

Page 95. Honokohau

Page 97. Akua Wahine

Page 99. Waikea- Ka ua Ke`oke`o -

Page 101. Ka Hekili a me Ka Huila

Page 103. Ko`u Ka Lā

Page 105. Hua Kapu`ole

Page 107. Ke Ke`oke`o Maoli

Page 109. Ho`opai I Ka Lani

Page 111. Ke Kiele Mae`ole

Page 113. E Ka Lani

Page 115. E KauhiWailani

Page 117. Ka Nani o `Īao

Page 119. No Ka Lani, no Ka Honua

Page 121. Pahumoa

Page 123. Ho`okahi Nō

Page 125. Ka `A`o Loko

Page 127. Nā Hōkū a me Ka Pō

Page 129. Ke Kumu Na`ena`e

Page 131. Mālamalama o Ka Mahina Kona

Page 133. Ke Moana, Ka `Ino, Ka Lā

Page 135. Kū, E Paniana

Page 137. Ka Pio Ke Ānuenue

Page 139. Ka Pua Mae`ole

Page 141. Ka Pua Rose

Page 143. Ka Makika

Page 145. OTHER TYPES OF POETRY
by Wayne Moniz

Page 147. Ku`u One Hānau (place)

Page 149-152. Ka Nene `Aukai o Kimo (travel)

Page 153. Wailuku 1957. (memory)

☆

Page 155. SONG LYRICS
by Wayne Moniz

Page 157-158. The Makawao 4th of July
Parade

Page 159. ORIGINAL SONG
FROM HIBISCUS POMADE

Page 161. Hibiscus Pomade.

Page 163. ORIGINAL SONGS
FROM STILL BORN:
NĀ MELE O KAHO`OLAWE
by Wayne Moniz

Page 165. Uē Kākou i Kēia Pō
Page 167. Ma Kela `Ao`ao Ke Ala
Page 169. He La`a Kea I Hele Kāua
Page 171-172. Ka Mele Kaumana o Ka
Mahina Maui

Page 173-174. Hide and Seek

Page 175-176. He Mele Hoena Hawai`i

Page 177-178. Hapa Haole Song circa
1941

Page 179. BONUS
A NEW POETIC DRAMA
By Wayne Moniz

Page 181. `ĪAO WHERE WE WALK
THROUGH RAINBOWS
`ĪAO, KAHI MĀ KOU E HELE
AI MA NĀ ĀNUENUE

Page 236. Poetic Drama Glossary

Page 237. Island Sites

Page 238-240. About Author and
purchases

CELEBRATIONS
OF
LIFE

Death ends a life,
Not a relationship.

Mitch Albon

DEDICATED TO
LARRY ENRIQUES

NĀ HUA`ŌLELO
(Vocabulary Words)

Ka Roselani - The Maui (heavenly) Rose
Wahikuli - Lahaina upland
Puali Nani- Wailuku area/sands of the area
Wailuku - Central Maui area
Keiki - buds/children
Haleakalā - 10,000 foot Maui volcano

KA ROSELANI
THE ROSELANI

Fair grows the rose
Of Wahikuli
Protected from the sweltering noon
In the shade of tall mango trees
And the clouds that skim off of the uplands
Unobtrusive, her fragrance
West winds blow her seeds over the mountain
Onto Puali Nani
The same clouds
That sheltered her at Wahikuli
Now protect her in Wailuku
Without the glare of the cruel sun
She flourishes
Her shrub bountiful with keiki
Blushed by the morning blessings
of Haleakalā
They inherit her soft barbs
She gazes in the face of a meandering stream
A complexion of pink innocence
Adding more beauty
to an already beautiful world.

NĀ HUA ʻŌLELO

Ka Panani o Ka Puna Hou – The Night Blooming
Cereus

ʻAuwai – waterway/ditch

Pā pōhaku – stone wall

Hongwanji – Japanese temple

KA PANINI O KA PUNA HOU
THE NIGHT-BLOOMING CEREUS

O special flower
Your arrival
Foreshadowed by perfume
The summer night warm
The moon full
The splashes in the `auwai
Stilled
Everything sensitive to your bloom
Rare magnificence
The glory of life
No matter how short
The matter how worthwhile
A double corona of yellow and white
Transforms the pā pōhaku
Mottled by a million stars
And the morning Hongwanji bells
Beat out slow, then fast, then faster
She starts to close
Her sensual beauty gone
Only memories wait
Wait to see her bloom again.

NĀ HUA`ŌLELO

Ke `Awapuhi - ginger
Kaleponi - California
Ke`oke`o - white
Pā`ia - East Maui area
Makani - winds
Agapanthus - blue blossoming, lily family,
                      flower
`Uki `uki - blue flowering berries used to dye
                  kapa cloth
Haina `ia mai ana ka puana (traditional) -
Telling the summary/refrain

KE `AWAPUHI
KE`O KE`O O KALEPONI
THE WHITE GINGER OF
CALIFORNIA

Driftwood descendant
Across the Pacific
The flower slip grows
Under the mountain's view
Where bowers of flowers bloom in the sun
The Child of Pā`ia
She evades the cold makani of winter
And thrives
Among the Agapanthus
Like the blue of the `uki `uki berry
Of her homeland
Three buds blossom
In white purity
Your perfume sanctifies the other plants
Sweet scent of Heaven
Ha`ina `ia mai ana ka puana
Of the White Ginger of California.

NĀ HUA ʻŌLELO

Haleakalā - Maui's 10,000 foot dormant volcano

Kapu - forbidden

Pili - a grass used for thatching

Hiʻiaka - the youngest sister of Pele, goddess of the volcano

KA MANAKŌ
THE MANGO

Hard to reach
That red-orange-golden one
That shines above the canopy
Haloed by the rays of Haleakalā
It's been there, ripening
Kapu even to the birds
Others have dropped to the ground
They repose in the pili grass
Covered by a spray of morning dew
Others are spotted
Too soft
Her flowers unique with red hairs
And now summer has come
It's time
The Grower approaches
Tenderly climbing the branched steps
Delicately he plucks
Carries down like Hi`iaka at the breast of Pele
Close to his bosom
Only a young one with a pure heart
With juices dripping
Will enjoy kā manakō.

NĀ HUA `ŌLELO

Mauna Kahālāwai - West Maui Mountains
Madeira - Portuguese Island, mid Atlantic.
(Many Madeirans came to work in Hawaii's
sugar fields.)
Kukui - Candlenut tree
`Iao - valley and stream, Central Maui

KA PUKANAWILA
THE BOUGAINVILLEA

Blushed
Like the sunsets
Poked by the jagged peaks
Of Mauna Kahālāwai
She could have been white, red, purple
But she is crimson
The color of passion and pain
A shoot once
A thriving bush now
Her full bracts
A tribute to beauty
Thorns bar her core
Her paper petals fall in the heat
A carpet created under her shade
For the weary not to worry
The flower that decorated Madeira's cliffs
And Wailuku's Valley of Kukui
Adorns the coal ground
And dreams the memories of a nourishing `Īao.

The Cherry Blossom is not an indigenous flower of Hawai`i but has a strong connection to the Hawai`i Japanese Community. It is one symbol in the multi-flowered lei of people who adorn Hawai`i Nei.

NĀ HUA `ŌLELO

Haru - (Japanese) Spring
U`i - beautiful
Makalapua - blossoming
Kahawai - stream

KA PUA KELI
THE CHERRY BLOSSOM

O fair flower
Announcer of the Haru
U`i indeed is Ka Pua Keli
Budding
Unveiling
Makalapua
Her pinks and whites brighten life
A bouquet on the top-most branch
Though tiny
She scents the surrounding grasses
At the end of Spring she drops
Whirling down into the kahawai
After her glory
She floats to her Source.

NĀ HUA ʻŌLELO

Lāʻau - tree
Lunalilo - lofty
Puʻu Kukui - Highest peak of Mauna Kahālāwai
Lāhainā - West Maui area
Maile - native shrub used for leis

KA PUAKENIKENI
THE TEN CENT FLOWER

Unique lā`au
Her blossoms bigger than the other puakenikeni
Large to bear the unending aloha
of her homeland - Maui
Nourished by the fine misty rain
of Mauna Kahālāwai
Towering lunalilo
She protects the life beneath
Three periods of a short but colorful life
First day - the white
Of billowy clouds over Pu`u Kukui
Second day - the yellow
Of the dawn painting Haleakalā
Third day - the orange
Of sunsets bathing Lāhainā
Her flowers blossom in the evening
Perfumed twilight
Now a fragrant pua of the night
Her spirited scent wins the heart
The Puakenikeni is twisted
Entwined by the maile

(Ka Puakenikeni continued next page)

When showers fall
Ha`ina `ia mai ana kapuana
Of the Grand Puakenikeni.

NĀ HUA `ŌLELO
(for opposite page Golden Lehua)

`Ōhi`a - tree with lehua blossoms
Ka`ala - mountain and area near Waipi`o, Big
        Island
Nā manu - birds
Wao kele - cloud forest
Napo`opo`o - Honaunau area of Big Island
Waimea - area north of Hilo
Hala - pandanus tree, leaves for weaving
Laka - goddess of the hula

KA LEHUA KULA O HAWAI`I NUI
THE GOLDEN LEHUA
OF HAWAI`I ISLAND

The skies cried
Its own precious flower was picked
Separated from her branch
Pele loved the `ōhi`a too late
She shook her stamen
Anointing the forest with honey dew
She came from the lone Lehua of Ka`ala
An attractive flower on the utmost branch
She came from a tree covered with nā manu
A tolerant towering evergreen
Thriving in the wao kele
Clinging along the ocean edge at Nāpō`opo`o
Her reflection in a fresh water pond of Waimea
Those far from Hawai`i
Inhaled the lehua mixed with the Maile and Hala
The precious flower of Heaven
Now adorns the altar of Laka
Haina `ia mai ana kapuana
A soft hymn
To Ka lehua Kula o Hawai`i Nui

NĀ HUA ʻŌLELO

Lokelani (Loke) (Roselani) - Maui rose.
Cleggan - Northwestern Ireland area
Marin - Northwestern San Francisco Bay area
Kīhei - South Maui area
Ka pua mahina - the flower moon

KA MAHINA LOKE
THE ROSE MOON

Blushed moon
Lokelani-hued
Seemingly sitting still in the western sky
Frame: Laced fringed delicate billows
Oh, gently coaxed crescent
You travel your arched path
Across the studded inky vastness
Jupiter joins you
And two glittered companions
Bask in your light
Your beam illuminates
Cleggan
The Headlands of Marin
And Maui's head
Simultaneously
From this spot on a strand of sand at Kīhei
Soon she outraces her stellar partners
She duplicates the rose lei pattern
Composed of a multitude of celestial bodies
Joyfully ka pua mahina is pulled
Along the circuitous path
Consoled that Jupiter and her moons
Will rejoin her after breaking Earth's shadow.

NĀ HUA ʻŌLELO

Mauna ʻEʻeka - Mauna Kahalawai/West Maui Mountains.

Lauhihi - plumbago

Pulelehua - butterfly

Violet Lake - source of water in Mauna Kahālāwai

Wai - water

KA LAUHIHI
THE PLUMBAGO

Mauna o `E`eka dominates
The last rays punctuate Maui's western peaks
Soon purple shadows will stain verdant valleys
Nature's pastel palette adds an imperial hue
The lauhihi
A feminine compliment to sea and sky
The powder blue of tranquility
Oh intertwined hedge magnet to pulelehua
A rainbow parade piloted by Common White,
Monarchs caped in sable and gold flutter past
To balance in the softness of her peace
Oh foreign flower
Your home is here now
Drought, wind, and heat are defied
You remain tolerant
Drink of the water not of battle
Drink of the pure from Violet Lake
Spill, sacred wai
Come nourish, flourish
In the rich soil of Wailuku.

NĀ HUA ʻŌLELO

Hanaiaʻeleʻele - ripening season for mountain apples

HinauluʻŌhʻiaʻai - pink around the blossom ends of the white mountain apple

Pele - goddess of volcanos

KA `ŌHI`A HO`OPALA I KA UA
THE RAIN RIPENED MOUNTAIN APPLE

Cheery Red
In a forest of stoic green
The forest flyers feast
They peck at your shiny coat
Sipping your sweet ambrosia
Your white blossoms Will yield bounty
So many will drop
When the sun is at its height
For it is the month of Hanaia`ele`ele
No need to strain, to stretch
To enjoy your company
Come rest on a carpet of scarlet blossoms
Your bark makes birthing facile
Inhale your sisters' scents: guava, eucalyptus
Pale is the ring of hinaulu `ōh`ia`ai
Pele's compeer
Not as large as the others of your kind
But small and plump hearts of cerise
Descendent of myrtle, Savor of pear
Oh patient fruit
Waiting for summer

(Apple continued on next page)

(Mountain Apple cont.)

When the hungry will relish
Your festival of red.

NĀ HUA `ŌLELO
(for opposite page)

Huluhulupue`o and Mananole Streams - water
source areas near Waiehu
Wai momona - sweet water
Lua `Eke - extinct crater in West Maui
               Mountains
Waihe`e - area north of Wailuku
Kealaka`I Honua and Haleki`i Pihana - heiau
(temples) near Waiehu
Puku Kalina - strong wind of the area
Jessamine - Vine with bright yellow flowers
               found in the Carolinas

KA PA`A MALE PAINA
THE IRONWOOD TREE COUPLE

Follow either Huluhulupue`o
Or Mananole Streams
They both rush wai momona from Lua `Eke
To nourish the ironwood at Waihe`e
The paina absorbs all
The aromatic branches, a berth
Rest in the arms of fallen pines
Listen to the wind whistle
Sweet dreamy tunes of peace.
Sacred this land of whispering conifers
Between Kealaka`i Honua and Haleki`i Pihana
Though twisted from the puku kalina
Its roots remain deep
Beneath the driftwood-studded shore
Occasionally a miracle occurs
A Jessamine is seen clinging to the pines
A flower that blooms holds such perfumes
As kindness and sympathy
Paina seeds have fallen along the beach
Soon a grove of green will soothe the new weary
Fresh rustles will again whir echoes
Of Aloha and Contentment.

NĀ HUA ʻŌLELO

Ānuenue - rainbow
Akua - God
Koʻolau - Windward Oʻahu mountain range
Nuʻuanu - Honolulu valley
Kaliuwaʻa - valley, Sacred Falls
Kāne - one of four great Hawaiian gods
Mānoa - valley mauka of Honolulu
Makapuʻu - beach near Koko Head, Oʻahu
Lanikai (Kaʻōhau) - beach near Kailua, Oʻahu
Kahalaopuna - the rainbow beauty of Mānoa
ʻAmakua - protector gods

KA LEI O NO`E
THE LEI OF MIST

Joy follows tears
Like a rainbow follows showers
So come, sweet ānuenue
Like Ke Akua's promise of love after deluge
Your reflection is everywhere
In the rain that strikes
the sheltering canopies of Honolulu
In the mists of the Ko`olau
In the fog of Nu`uanu
In the water of Kaliuwa`a
In the moonbow over Waikīkī
Oh, perch of Kāne
We praise your colors
The red, orange, and yellow of roses, of orchids
Of the turning leaves before the cold of winter
The green of the twisting kukui in Mānoa
The blue of the rushing waves at Makapu`u
The indigo of twilight above Diamond Head
The violet of the sunrise over Lanikai
Oh Rose of Rainbows
Yours is the beauty of Kahalaopuna
Our multicolored `amakua
Give us hope
When tears fall like rain.

NĀ HUA ʻŌLELO

Lāhui - species
Hōkūloa - The Evening Star, Venus
Pukana Lā - sunset
Lokelani - the Maui rose
Ke anuʻenuʻe - the rainbow
Iho - core
Puʻuʻulaʻula - red sands of Haleakalā
ʻŌhelo berry - shrub cranberry family, sacred to
                          Pele
Koko - blood
Waimea - red water
Pumehana - warmth

KA PUA HUELO
THE ANTHURIUM

Of the myriad of her lāhui
This Pua Huelo flourishes exclusively
She is not the white of Hōkūloa
She is not the orange of pukana lā
She is not the pink of the Lokelani
She is not the divers colors of ke anu`enu`e
Her iho, her core
Redder than the sands of Pu`u`ula`ula
Redder than the `ōhelo berry
Redder than the koko of her `ohana
She is born of waimea,
Her waxed heart was transplanted
Farthest from the Earth's core
To Haleakalā, the House of the Sun
Her Maui mountain echoes stories
Of her winsomeness
Ka pumehana of this singular anthurium
Attracts all
Her delicate flower feeds them
The memory of her beauty endures
Ha`ina `ia mai ana kapuana
Ka Pua Huleo o Maui.

NĀ HUA ʻŌLELO

Aliʻi - chiefs
ʻUki grass - coarse sedge
Kāhili - standard of royalty
Moku - island
Lokelani - Maui's pink rose
Ka Pua Kalikimaka - poinsettia
Kepaniwai - area in ʻĪao Valley

KA `AWAPUHI `ULA `ULA O `ĪAO
THE RED GINGER OF `ĪAO

She claims common
But she adorns the Ali`i
Her blossoms celebrate birth
Mourns death
Witnesses aloha
E `Awapuhi `ula `ula
Your blood red blooms sway
As the leaves of kukui flutter
The blades of the `uki grass wave to and fro
Mauna Kahālāwai's stream splashes
E Kāhili of the Garden
You hold court
With our moku's pink Lokelani
You plead for the slanted rains to baptize
For the wheat to grow
In preparation for your winter sister
Ka Pua Kalikimaka
Oh, tolerant flower
Lingering in the half shade
Like all, tips burn, the casualties of life
But your ruby rhizomes are robust

(The Red Ginger continued on next page.)

(Red Ginger cont.)

You last longer than the others
In this hallowed ground
Below the towering cliff faces of Kepaniwai.
Your bracts extend to subtle precious white floret
From you come issues of new life
Like your ancestors
You grace pathways that lead to uplands
We remember your admonition:
E hihi ka helena i ka uka o `Iao
Take on your way back
If not spoiler rains will come
Haina `ia mai ana kapuana
Ke `Awapuhi `Ula `Ula o `Iao.

NĀ HUA `ŌLELO
(for opposite page red carnation lei)

Kui - sew
Pā`ia - East Maui area
Kahului - Maui Central Plain area
Pukalani - area on slopes of Haleakalā
La`au niu. - palm fronds
Kālua - double strand lei
Hanana - event
Pakalana, plumeria, pīkake - local flowers
Nā hali`a aloha eha hōkū - stardust memories

46

KA LEI PONIMŌ`Ī `ULA KĀLUA
THE DOUBLE RED CARNATION LEI

They are petals of passion
Come kui her buds
She grew heartily in
Pāi`a
Kahului
Pukalani
Come string memories of aloha
Balmy nights
Twilight Shadows
Blue Hawaii
Moonbeams gleam on the la`au niu.
The lei is strung
By laughter In the night
Oh Sweet Lei
Rarely given
No single strand tonight
Kālua for a special hanana.
Her double strand lei
Is firm but soft
Soft but firm.

(Double Red Carnation lei
Continued on next page.)

She'll outlast the night and
The pakalana
The plumeria
The pīkake.
In the morning she remains richly red
Red as the cheeks of her keiki.
Ha`ina `ia mai ana kapuana
Nā hali`a aloha ehu hōkū
O Ka Lei Ponimō`ī `Ūla Kālua.

NĀ HUA `ŌLELO
(for opposite page Ka `Ukulele)

Laka - goddess of the forest
Kumu - tree
`Elepaio - bird, if not seen, sign of a healthy tree
Pā`ia - area of East Maui
Piko - navel/the core/source
Leo - voice

KA `UKULELE
THE JUMPING FLEA

From the seed, Laka has nourished Ke Koa
Forged and shaped by other gods
Of wind and rain, lightning and thunder, and
sun
The Majestic Kumu calls out
"Take me from the three tiered canopy
The `elepaio is absent"
Lono cries,
"You are the Chosen One,
Retrieved from mid-forest
On the slopes above Pā`ia"
The god of music shapes
The passionate curves of his woman
Thankful for her nourishment and love
He carves her neck long and sensual
Rounds her piko for strains of birth.
Melodies are plucked from her.
She is the medium to the god of music
Tuned in the key of Aloha.
Her leo echo from the slopes of Haleakalā
To the valleys of Mauna Kahālāwai,
The mele of bliss and blues and Hawai`i Nei.
(Jumping Flea continued on next page.)

(Jumping Flea cont.)

She sits in the corner now
Having been played out.
The sun is setting in the Lāhaina Sea
Lā gilds the fading finish
Time for the ha`ina:
Remember the joyful strums
Of our beloved instrument of Aloha.

NĀ HUA `ŌLELO
(for opposite page The Whale)

Fluke - either side of the whale's tail
Huila - wheels
Mele - song
I ka pō - in the night

KE KOHOLĀ
THE WHALE

Cheery hearted traveler
Maui's warm water welcomes
Your permanent homecoming
Oh strong swimmer
Gifted flippers fluke
Nā Huila of the sea
Oh giant of gentility
Sing your magic mele
The sounds of
New and earned life In harmony
With playful porpoises now
With all ancestors joined
Splashes heard I ka pō
It is the spirit of largeness
It is the whisper of finesse
In the ocean of imagination.

NĀ HUA'ŌLELO

Pāpio - young stage of ulua
Pelagic - fish of the sea
'Ōama - young of the weke, goat fish

KA ULUA
THE TREVALLY

All creatures of the sea
Pay homage to the ulua
Commoner as pāpio
Royalty as elders
Lustrous kingfish
Independent sojourner
Of sparkling splinter in an undersea cloud
The evasive one grows
His security preserved in the maze of lava reef
Or in shadow of shark or seal
Pursued pelagic
Or pursuer of `oama
Flying fish in the shallows
Governed by the silver moon
Shimmering the surface of a midnight lagoon.

NĀ HUA ʻŌLELO

Onaga – Japanese for ʻulaʻula
Iāpana – Japan
Lokelani – Maui rose

KA `ULA`ULA
THE RED SNAPPER

E, gem of the sea
Ruby of the deep
Celebrating the journey of twelve moons
E `ula `ula of Hawai`i Nei
E Onaga o `Iāpana
Your red dorsal joins sea to sky
How deep is the plunge
To the dark of depth
Where the prize thrives among
A universe of starfish
Shunner of burnt flesh
He retreats to the summer in hibernation
To grow and paint the sea pink in winter
The tint of the Lokelani.

NĀ HUNA `ŌLELO

Kaupō - area East Maui
`Ōpū - stomach
Ali`i - royalty
Kapu - forbidden
Keiki - child

KA MOI
THE THREADFISH

Kaupō is dark now
When the dawn breaks in the eastern sea
The chop will give way to a brief calm
Hurry to the ko`a, the secret feeding spot
Come view the sacred moi
Do not seize the adults
It was only for the `ōpū of the ali`i
Kapū to the keiki
Ignorant of the moon's phases
I spot the red-eyed one
It is a four pounder
One that can now be shared
with the ali`i and me.

NĀ HUNA ʻŌLELO

Singing snails - tree snails that make sounds

ʻEmoloa - Hawaiian grass

Kolea Kai Piha - seaside vegetation

E ʻai kākou - come eat

Tuusiik - the sound associated with bobbing by
       Alaskan natives

ʻĀlaka - Alaska

Kūnou - the sound associated with bobbing by
       Hawaiian natives

Noddy - head

KE KŌLEA
THE PACIFIC GOLDEN PLOVER

The singing snails announce
A deity is among us
Ke Kolea is a flyer
Who returns to feed in the high `emoloa
Or kōlea kai piha along the shore
Oh message bearer to the ali`i
Do not circle my home
Instead, E `ai kākou!
Let us eat, Celebrate before you depart
The Wandering Tattler your travel companion
Brags of your golden Plover feathers
Tuusiik! Tuusiik! lures `Ālaka
Time to leave your crescent shoreline
The tide has risen
Kūnou! Kūnou!
Bobbing your noddy
A prelude to flight.

NĀ HUNA ʻŌLELO

Porto Moniz - seaport southern Madeira Island
Makela - Hawaiian for Madeira
Cercial - Wine from the Porto Moniz region
Poios - terraces
Tintanegramole - most abundant grape of
                                    Madera
Māla kō - sugar cane fields
Ka eʻe moku - immigrant
Maka waina - vineyard
Puhali - birthing sands near Wailuku
ʻAnuhea - cool/sweet
Paʻi waina - cluster of grapes
Nō ka ʻoi - the best
ʻAhaʻaina - wedding feast
Iesū - Jesus
Nā pahu - the casks
Koko - blood
Waina - wine
ʻIlihune - poor
Hoʻolauleʻa - celebration

KA HUA WAINA
FRUIT OF THE VINE

The scent of almonds tumbles
Down the hills above Porto Moniz
Gambols into Makela's Coast Winds
How salty the Cercial
How dry the taste for palates
In distant lands
The surrounding poios bulge
With tintanegramole.
On ships, aging onward
Nā Hua o Vancouver a me Marin
On other ships, to work nā māla kō
Ka e`e cradled his vintage relic
From the Old World
His inconspicuous pua huddled in the hold
Like Hi`iaka at the breast of Pele
One day there will be wine
E Maui, hua waina flourishes
Your warm sun, your trades mimic Makela
You now gild the slopes of Haleakalā
And the smaller maka waina in Wailuku
Puhali Nani's fertile sands
`Īao's `anuhea and nourishing stream
The fresh trades from Pa`ia:
(Fruit of the Vine continued on next page.)

(Fruit of the Vine cont.)
All comprise the formula for
Ka waina's honored recipe
Now comes pa`i waina
Harvested, crushed, pressed
Fermented in oak casks
20-100 years nō ka `oi.
The `aha`aina at Canaan
Resumes celebrating the couple's bond
Iesū has refilled nā pahu
The same whose koko is waina
Don't glean the harvest
Invite the `ilihune to the ho`olaule`a!
Come celebrate Abundance, Fertility
Good luck And Re-birth.

NĀ HUNA `ŌLELO
(for opposite page sugar cane)

Ki - ti leaf
`Ulu - breadfruit
Mai`a - banana
Niu - coconut
`Uala- sweet potato
Nā lau kō - sugar cane leaves
kilohōkū - star gazer
Luna - boss, above
Pu`ukoli`i - area above Lāhainā
Kilepalepa poni - cane tassels

KE KŌ O PU`UKOLI`I
THE SUGAR CANE OF PU`UKOLI`I

He came with ki, `ulu, mai`a, niu, `uala,
and kalo.
The long journey from beneath the long clouds
The canoe slaps at aggressor waves
Nā lau kō flap green in the trades
A flag of health and life
Kilohōkū sees in dreams
Valleys and plains
To plant the Kō.
How hard the little plot growing Kō
After the grape blight
Until foreigners came to Makela
Came for recruits for the sugar plantations
Wanderlust and wealth
Lured them to the Sandwich Isles.
Gone are the potatoes
Kō has now dominated Lāhainā
He is luna above all
Surrounded by his fellow brothers
He has proliferated
His tassels wave to the towering mango trees
Of Pu`ukoli`i.

(The Sugar Cane of Pu`ukoli`i cont.)

(Sugar Cane of Pu`ukoli`i cont.)

And now after maturity
Before the fields are set ablaze
His shoots are imbedded
In Wailuku's inviting soil.
It's time to rest, to listen
To the whispering composer
The Kīlepalepa poni blossoms strum tunes
About peace, contentment.
He sleeps and dreams
Of new valleys and plains
To plant the Kō.

NĀ HUNA `ŌLELO
(for opposite page the taro)

Wai - water
Lo`i - taro patch
Keiki - child
Waihe`e - Area north of Wailuku
Kukui - candlenut tree
Welo - month in the moon calendar
Pua`a - pig, pork
Kealakaihonua - Waihe`e heiau (temple)
Mauna Alani - mountain above Waihe`e

KE KALO
THE TARO

The peace of the flowing wai of the Lo`i
The kalo stands rooted
In the soil of its ancestors
The native of generations
Oh, big leaved fish of the land
No bones this food for keiki
Content this kalo in his own place
Listen to the whispers, the winds of Waihe`e
The voices of the bitter purple plum branches
The turning of the kukui leaves, green, white
The journey is long the kalo light
Oh simple sustenance
Now is Welo, the time for planting
The rains are ripe
When mature
An offering as precious as pua`a
At Kealakaihonua at the sea
And to your back
The misty Mauna Alani.

NĀ HUNA ʻŌLELO

Paiʻea - Another name for Kamehameha the
       Great

Nani ʻena ʻena - glowing beauty

Hoʻi mai hou - return again

KA HŌKŪ WELOWELO
THE SHOOTING STAR

You came quickly
A shooting star
In the night
I noticed you, shining
But I paid more attention
To others needs
And when I looked back
You were gone
I was foolish
To have not spent more time enjoying you
You will return
Within a lifetime
Like ka hōkū of Pai`ea
Haina `ia mai ana kapuana
I saw your nani `ena `ena
Ho`i mai hou.

NĀ HUA `ŌLELO

Koa - Acacia tree/warrior

Kilakila - majestic

Kāne - one of the great Hawaiian gods

Kalapana - area, Puna, Hawai`i Nui

Kalehua - area, Puna

Nā Wai `Ehā - The Four Streams, Maui

Pali - cliffs

Kapalehua and A`alaloa - the boundaries of
Waiehu

Waikele - forest

Māke - dead

Moku - island

hā - breath

KE KOA
THE KOA TREE

Kilakila o ke koa
Voices brag of your strength
Your seed issued in the bosom of Kāne
Pulled tight
By the reclining coconut trees at Kalapana
You frolicked at Kalehua
A dream drifting to Kailua
Then off to the land of Nā Wai `Ehā
Rooted between the Pali o Kapalehua
A me A`alaloa
Your towering branches shield,
Protect all under your shade
In the sear of summer, the whips of winter
Your scattered seeds are later barks imagined
Ke Koa's life does not end in the Waikele
The fallen tree is not māke
He is shaped into a voyager
Heading for that island
That appears in swirling mists
Similar to the beauty of those islands
He was rooted in
Except now, a moku without strife
He is greeted by those waiting for him
With the sweet hā of love.

NĀ HUA `ŌLELO

Ka`ahumanu - Kamehameha the Great's Queen
Pi`ilani - chief who constructed Maui's roads.
Maka`āinana - commoners
Kā`uiki - hill above Hāna/famous warrior.
`Awapuhi ke`oke`o - white ginger
Ka`eokalani - legendary Hāna character
Ehu kai - sea scent
Mālualua - North Wind
Hāmoa - Hāna beach, surf spot
Mālie - calm
Kaihuokala - mountain above Hāna
Aokū - rainclouds
Pu`uki`i - island off of Hāna
Lau niu - coconut leaves

KA UA KE`OKE`O O HĀNA
THE WHITE RAIN OF HĀNA

Oh, land of Ka`ahumanu, of Pi`ilani
Of the maka`āiana
Come climb the hill Kā`uiki calls
For one last time.
Come listen to the rain
On the `awapuhi ke`oke`o
Drip rhythmically
And create perfume for angels
The son of Ka`eokulani
Pierces the banana leaf
Not the sky, not with spear, but with song
Oh, humble rain, nature's baptism
You refresh anew
Come mix with the `ehu kai
Wafting from the bay
The Mālualua will carry you to cool Hāmoa
The strings in my heart
Slacken with your aloha
Echo the sounds of ancestors
Wānanalua is the land
Punahoa is the pond
Kā`uiki is the hill
Ka Uakea o Hāna is the mele

(White Rain continued on next page)

(The White Rain of Hāna cont.)

The tears fall, the clouds weep
Nevertheless tomorrow - mālie Hāna
For Kaihuokala will be clearly seen
Every time aokū gather over Pu`uki`i
And drops strum its lau niu
Remember Ka Ua Kea o Hāna.

NĀ HUA `ŌLELO
(for opposite page/ Lehua)

Lehua - flower of the `ōhi`a tree
`Ōla`a - area of Kīlauea, Hawai`i Nui
Pana`ewa - forest area near Hilo
Kapa (tapa) - material made from the wauke
                bark
Pai`ea - Kamehameha the Great
Koko - blood
Mayflower - U.S. East Coast bloom

LEHUA MAU LOA
EVERLASTING LEHUA

`Ōla`a is darkened by the smoke of the land
Even Pele mourns sheds red lehua rain
The young one weaves his way
Through the dogwood maze
Unlike the peaceful paths through Pana`ewa
The rainforest named by the demi-god
Who protected him in his homeland
But distant battle will shape the kapa beaters
Into weapons and gunwales
He will fight, he comes from great warriors
Protectors of Pai`ea
The red star reflects the koko
Hilo is proud
Come sew the first buds of lehua
The first buds of mayflower
Come make a lei for his sacrifice.

NĀ HUA ʻŌLELO

Ke Kanaka Luʻu i ka Hohonu - merman

Maui and Hina - husband and wife, parents of ʻĪao

Kapu - forbidden

ʻĪao - daughter of Maui and Hina/ valley, stream, Central Maui

Kuʻuipo - loved one

Puʻuokamoa - another name for ʻĪao's love, the merman

Truckee - river in Yosemite

Guadalupe - river in south San Francisco Bay

KE KANAKA LU`U
i KA HOHONU PŌHAKU
THE STONE MERMAN

The verdant monolith stands mighty
Towering over all
His head in the billowy clouds
Haloed in an aura of blue
His base surrounded
By the greens and browns of Earth.
The majestic justice of Maui and Hina
Greets all to the valley,
Because of their kapu love
`Īao now in eternal awe
Gazes upward at her ku`uipo,
The merman, Pu`uokamoa.
How she yearned for his glistening arms
How they kissed in dark wet shadows
A sensual hide and seek
In the grove of kukui.
It is said that his pelagic odyssey
Went beyond Maui's streams
And across the Pacific
His underwater shadow
Traversed the Truckee

(Stone Merman Continued on next page)

(The Stone Merman cont.)

Wandered the Guadalupe.
The Wailuku River gives him nourishment
The artery of koko that keeps him eternal.
Let the story be told
Of Pu`uokamoa
In the Yosemite of the Pacific.

NĀ HUA `ŌLELO
(for opposite page)

Lā`au `ula `ula - redwood

Sierra Nevada - mountain chain, Northeastern
California

Chetco - Southwestern Oregon river

Siskiyou - coast subrange of Klamath
Mountains, Oregon

Santa Lucia - Coastal mountain range, Central
California

Alta California - old name for Northern
California

Murrelet -Small Pacific Coast seabird/nests in
old forests

KA LĀ`AU `ULA`ULA O KALEPONI
THE CALIFORNIA REDWOOD

He still lives
After 2000 years
In a sash of Lā`au `ula `ula
That fringes the land of gold.
The pure aqua nourishes, spills
Out of the Sierra Nevada
And tumbles from the Chetco River
In the Siskiyou Mountains
Slithering south to the Santa Lucia
Into Monterey Bay.
The mighty Redwood,
Indigenous sentinel
Of the Alta California shoreline,
Gazes down upon the poised Pacific
A placidity for oysters and otters.
He's tall, perhaps 300 feet
Fires only slightly singe him
The Peleated Woodpecker knocks
To check on him
The Marbled Murrelet Is cradled
In his evergreen sleeves
The Spotted Owl embraces his limbs.

(California Redwood continued on next page)

(The California Redwood cont.)

A female Black-tailed Deer
Has declared home
Under his canopy
She is shielded in shade
Protected from predators
Now the call of distant sea birds
Announce the setting sun
Fog will soon be slinking down
The golden-poppied hills
The mist will soothe the California Redwood
He will sleep in its ethereal arms.

NĀ HUA `ŌLELO
(for next two pages/Moku lua)

Moku Nui and Moku Iki - two tiny islands off
Lanikai Beach, O`ahu
Ka`ōhao - Hawaiian name for Lanikai Beach
Lua Pele - volcano
`Ākulikuli ... etc. endemic shrubs and flowers
Hulu - feathers/ esteemed person
`U`au kani - wedged-tail shearwater
Mano - shark
Lōlī`i - rest

NĀ MOKU LUA
THE TWO ISLANDS

Ka`ōhao gazes at Moku Nui and Moku Iki
To her he is one
One open to the world
To life carried in by the trades
The other preserved for the future
Ka`ōhao's crescent shawl of sand
Gazes across the way to the body and soul
of Nā Mokulua
The woman of the white garment
created him three million years ago
He is the heart of Lua Pele
The Ko`olau shields him from humid Kona
All of the beauty of the islands
Is in this one twin:
Sheer cliffs, a sandy beach
Crashing waves, the blues of heaven
He is suited in the finest:
`Ākulikuli, alena, naupaka, `aki`aki
Pua kala, `ilima, `emoloa,, `āweoweo
He is esteemed
Draped by the hulu of the `u`au kani
The mano of ancestors protect him
He is a repose for the monk seal

(Two Islands continued on next page)

Lōli`i also for the weary In a luminescent
Unique teal waterway with underwater gems
Come, stare at the sky
Float along its aqueous path
And when the sun rises directly
Between Nā Mokulua
And the full moon rises
Between the body and soul
Haina `ia mai ana kapuana
Of the birth and future of Nā Mokulua.

BIRTHDAYS

In the ancient days of Hawai`i,
a baby's first birthday was celebrated.
The boy or girl had passed a crucial period
without illness.
The first three kaona of this section
were written for three babies
to commemorate their good health.
Sometimes there are
other special birthdays
that deserve a kaona
like Lucile Mistysyn's 100th birthday.

NĀ HUA ʻŌLELO

Waiehu - area near Wailuku
Laha ʻole - unique
Roselani - Maui Island's pink flower

KA AO `ĀKALA MO`ONI
THE PINK SPIRAL CLOUD

A pink spiral cloud
Appears over Waiehu
Laha `ole
In contrast to Haleakala's blue
A puffy top
The color of the roselani
A joyful toy
Hovering over
The sky's mirror
When dark clouds invade
Haina `ia mai ana kapuana
O Ka Ao `Ākala Mo`oni.

NĀ HUA`ŌLELO

Pilali - sap of the kukui
Waihe`e - area north of Wailuku
Kalo - taro, plant used for making poi.
Ke`anae - East Maui area

HE LEI KAMALI`I
A CHILD LEI

A beloved one
Fondled in the arms
Carried on the back
Arms around the neck like a lei
A lei never forgotten is the child
A summer lei
A winter lei
Is the child
Steadfast like the Pilali gum
Sticks to the kukui
Inviting like the sea scent at Waihe`e
Sweet like the kalo of Ke`anae
A lei that is never set aside
Is one's child.

NĀ HUA ʻŌLELO

ʻEhu kai - sea scent
Līpoa - seaweed
ʻŌʻō - extinct black and yellow honey eater bird
Mamo - black honeycreeper, also extinct
Mele - sing
Kaʻiulani - Princess wife of King David
          Kalākaua
Kawika (David) - Hawaiian name of King David
          Kalākaua
Heiau - temple

KAULANA `OE,
E KA PUA PĪKAKE
YOU ARE FAMOUS,
OH PEACOCK BLOSSOM

Kaulana `oe, e ka pua pīkake
The gift of the gods
Who bathed in your perfume
And the savor of sandalwood
Your pearls are gathered at dusk for lei
The `ehu kai
Nudges the sweet scent of līpoa
To mingle with your fragrance of love
The peacocks, the `ō`ō, the mamo compliment
They mele in your garden shade
You are Ka`iulani
Whose fond savor fuses with the rose
Revered one daughter of Kawika
You dwell in the highest point of Heaven
You adorn the entrance to heiau
You are sacredness
Purity
Simplicity
Sincerity
Ha`ina `ia mai ana kapuana
Ka Pua Pīkake Kaulana.

NĀ HUA ʻŌLELO

ʻIwalani - frigate bird

Kaʻau Crater - caldera above Pālolo Valley

Waimao and Pūkele - streams that join to create
Pālolo Stream

Pālolo - valley/stream above Kaimuki, Oʻahu

Kāne and Kanaloa - two of the most important
gods

Kalaepohaku - St. Louis Heights

Ahupuaʻa - land area usually from mountain to
the sea

Waiʻanae - mountain range, Oʻahu

Akua - God

KA PUA MELIA
O MAKALEKA KAMIKA
THE PLUMERIA OF
MARGARET SMITH

A lone `Iwalani
Pierces the clouds
Ka`au Crater fills
Its aquifers gush with glee
Her fill tumbles
And slides down seven waterfalls
Waimao meets Pūkele and they beget Pālolo
The water given by Kāne and Kanaloa
Nourishes the white ginger
Baptizes the towering wild plum
The genuflecting fern
Splashes the stepping stones
That lead to the terraces of Kalaepohāku
A rainbow mist - Lehopulu- veils the ahupua`a
There she is!
Air-brushed with blush
Like the skies above the Wai`anae
Glossed white
like the foaming crests of distant Waikīkī
Amidst the foliage of Akua's Hawaiian Eden
The descendent of Ka Melia Makaleka Kamika

(Smith Plumeria continued on next page)

(Plumeria continued from previous page)

Come celebrate her beauty
Come celebrate her sweet scent
Ha`ina `ia mai ana ka puana
Ka Pua Melia O Makaleka.

DEDICATION

(IN THE ORDER OF THEIR KAONA)

MARGARET TEXEIRA MONIZ 17
MARY TEXEIRA TORRES 19
LUCILLE MONIZ COELHO 21
RUSTY MONIZ BIDDIX 23
MARIE MONIZ STEELEY 25
PAT YANAGI MONIZ 27
ALEXA SANTOS KAHUI 29,30
NONA DESHA BEAMER 31
ANNA O'TOOLE ASPELL 33
JOACHINA MARTINS TEXEIRA 35
IDA RODRIGUES MONIZ 37,38
CHUCK & MARLENE POWELL 39
CHARLOTTE HANAKO ONNA 41
RUTHIE DEPONTE 43
MARGARET DUARTE 45,46
PAULETTE SOUZA DAVIS 47,48
PENNY DAVIS 49,50
CLARENCE BUTCH MONIZ 51
STAN MONIZ 53
STEVE MONIZ 55
EDDIE MONIZ 57
JOHN MONIZ 59
DIOGO MONIZ 61,62
ANTONE TEXEIRA 63,64
JOHNNY TEXEIRA 65
KAMUELA KAHUI 67
JEROME KELIIHOOMALU 69
PEKELO COSMA 71,72
HENRY HOOLULU PITMAN 73

(DEDICATION CONT.)

GLENN AWAI 75
TOM DANKWARDT 77,78
RUSSELL COELHO 79,80
CASSIE SMITH 83
MARLEY SMITH 85
KIANI KAHUI 87
LUCILE SMITH MISTYSYN 89,90

NĀ KAONA FROM MY FRIENDS

DEDICATED TO LES KULOLOIO

I learned about kaona and decided
to teach it to the students
in my Writing classes.
I noticed the sophistication
of those who wrote kaona
versus the Hallmark School of Writing
(I love you, you love me,
let's sit under the papaya tree).
I saw the impact of kaona
when my students
including special ed students
started winning writing contests.
The judges noted their
elegant, mature style.
Here are some of their alluring kaona.

NĀ HUA`ŌLELO

Honokōhau - highest waterfall in Mauna
                Kahālawai (West Maui Mountains)
Waiehu - beachside area, near Wailuku, North
        Maui
Makana - gift
Maui - demigod who pulled up the islands

WAILELE HONOKŌHAU
HONOKŌHAU WATERFALL

In the dark before the dawn
Honokōhau roughly breaks the surface
Agitating the calm pond
Absorbed by the unwinding stream
Passing from Kano Olewa, the rain magnet
To the high tide at Waiehu's shore
Its backdrop, the burnt orange makana
Of Maui's snare.

Lizelle Soriano

NĀ HUA ʻŌLELO

ʻAina - land
Nani - beautiful
Akaaka - clear/glass
Kalo - taro
Hiamoe - sleeping
Moʻo - lizard
Aʻa - rough lava

AKUA WAHINE
GODDESS

The `aina, nani
The ocean, akaaka wale
The Kalo, sweet
The clouds, skimming
The sun, in place
Ready to set, hiamoe
Haleakala, quiet
She's at peace
Do not disturb her
She'll roar like a deranged mo`o
Spitting her bloodied a`a
Ending in a beginning.

Shandell Park

NĀ HUA ʻŌLELO

Lono - god of fertility, agriculture
Ka hulu - feathers

WAIKEA - KA UA KEOKEO
WAIKEA - THE WHITE RAIN

Lono greens the `aina
Gentle as ka hulu of the honey creeper
Falls hard then stops
Falls again stops
Suddenly a deluge
The flash flood churns the river.

Courtnie Arcanado

NĀ HUA `ŌLELO

Ka Hekili - thunder
Ka Uila - lightning
Silversword - succulent that grows on and in
                  Haleakalā Crater
`Ō`ō - black honey eater

KA HEKILI A ME KA UILA
THE THUNDER AND THE
LIGHTNING

Piercing hard the dark cold night
Scary strikes of a thousand knives
Crackling silver across Haleakalā
Gleamed in Elmo's green
Roaring, fear raising
The leaves of the Silversword quivering
The `Ō`ō seeks shelter from a fiery bolt
Cruel and mysterious
O ka hekili a me ka uila.

Dawn Dunstan

NĀ HUA `ŌLELO

Aloha Kakahiaka - good morning
Pumehana - warmth/affection
Pō - night/darkness
Kukui - lamp
Mālama - care

KO`U LĀ
MY SUN

Aloha kakahiaka, e Sun!
Embraced by sister clouds
Blessing with Pumehana
Overpowering my darkness a black like Pō
The heaven's kukui lit my path
Too much light sometimes blurs my vision
Mālama flickers.

Kristi Tintiangco

NĀ HUA ʻŌLELO

Mauna Kahālāwai - West Maui Mountains
Pili - grass used for thatching

HUA KAPU`OLE
UNFORBIDDEN FRUIT

High on Mauna Kahālāwai
Lives a spreading Indian mango tree
Nestled under its verdure leaved canopy
Her branches shade, shield, assure
At her feet traces of fallen sunburst eggs
Repose in the pili grass
Oh Provider dripping juices tell how sweet.

Lynel Dimapasoc

NĀ HUA ʻŌLELO

Hāna - area, East Maui
Makana - gift
Manu - bird
Pueo keʻokeʻo - white owl
Nahiku - area, East Maui
ʻŌheʻo - stream, East Maui
Mahina - moon

KA MAOLI KE`O KE`O
WHITE NATIVE

The white owl departs
Soaring over Hāna through the dark
Alternating between mountain and sea
Blessed with the makana of flight
The shape of the good-hearted manu
Reflect off of Nahiku's moonlit waterfalls
Like a tranquil comet
Pueo ke`oke`o
Like the white rain showers
Over the pools of `Ōhe`o
The winds bolster her
Leaving a silhouette against
The silver mahina
Settled
The nocturnal aviator
Envisions the next night
And prepares.

Mariatani Swope

NĀ HUA `ŌLELO

Ho`opa - touch

Kū - stand firm

Niu - coconut tree

Makuahine - mother

Mālamalama. - caring

Lahaina Noon - When sun is directly above/ no
shadow

Mea - thing

Pu`u o Ka Moa - Another name for `Īa`o Needle

HO`OPA I KA LANI
TOUCHING HEAVEN

Standing strong, though storm stripped,
Beaten, weathered like the ironwood
At Waihe`e
Kū, e Niu!
Your milk nourishes ,
E makuahine mālamalama
Your fronds adumbrate Lahaina Noon
E spindly waisted mea hula
Thrusting like `Iao's Pu`u o Ka Moa.

Shayna Carroll

NĀ HUA ʻŌLELO

ʻAʻala - scent
Ka māla - the garden

KE KIELE MAE`OLE
THE NEVER FADING GARDENIA

E Kiele never fading flower
Sweet and soft `a`ala
Gentle and smooth petals
Peacefully soaking up the sun
Natural beauty of ka māla
Ka Pua Mae`ole.

Sasha Gomez

NĀ HUA `ŌLELO

Ka hekili a me ka uila. - thunder and lightning
Ko`olau - mountain range, O`ahu
`Imihau - strong winds of Lahaina
Pāpa`a Lā - winds with showers, East Maui
Kamehameha pōhākū - The lonely One's rock/
                                    legend of his strength
Mai`a - banana

NĀ LANI
THE HEAVENS

Strong like ka hekili a me ka uila
Soft like the gentle Ko`olau currents
Breaks like the `Imihau winds
That topple koa
Comforting like the balmy breeze -
Pāpa`a Lā
Like the stubborn immovable
Kamehameha pōhāku
Sweet as the Mai`a blossom
Mysterious as the Southern Cross.

Chanelle Awana

NĀ HUA ʻOLELO

Kula - area in Upcountry Maui
Puʻu ʻUlaʻUla - red sands of Haleakalā
Lio - horse

E KAUHIWAILANI
OH HEAVENLY MIST

He gallops Kula's wide pastures
His muscles tighten and tug
Heaven's Equus sparkles
Bathed by the breezes from Pu`u `ula`ula
Wafting through the eucalyptus
Sentinel of the foal
Lio, strider of Eternity's Fields.

Sherilynn Kaniho

NĀ HUA ʻŌLELO

Maluhia - peaceful
Anuhea - sweet
Wai - water
pōhākū - boulders
Noho māliʻe - peaceful place
Mahina - moon
Palu kukui - stars
Mele - song
Makani - wind
He lani I luna - the sky above
He Honua I lalo - the earth below

KA NANI O ʻĪAO
THE BEAUTY OF ʻĪAO

Maluhia ka wai of ʻĪao Stream
The anuhea of sweet guava lingers
The inviting pōhākū, stepping stones
To the noho māliʻe
Still radiant during the day
The silvery mahina
Hanging from
The palu kukui-kissed ceiling
Honey creepers sing an ancient mele
Whispers of the gentle makani
Tell tales of blood and peace
He lani i luna, he honua i lalo.

Jenna McKown

NĀ HUA ʻŌLELO

Noho I ka lani - stay in the heavens
Pueo - owl
Waikiʻi - area Hawaiʻi Nui
ʻAuhea wale - mild command to listen
Ua - rain
Anela - angel
Hale - home

NO NĀ LANI, NO KA HONUA
FOR THE HEAVENS,
FOR THE EARTH

Noho I ka lani, e Pueo
Within the fine mist of Waiki`i pastures
Protect, guide, observe
E`auhea wale `oe i ka ua
Soar Anela
To your hale in the sky
I'll miss you, my pueo
No nā lani, no ka Honua
Guardian of Heaven and Earth.

Ariel Pacleb

NĀ HUA ʻŌLELO

Lāʻie - area near Kahuku, Oʻahu
Maka hinahina - silver-like foliage found along
                        shorelines
Koʻolau - mountain range, Oʻahu
ʻUa - rain
Nalu - waves

PAHUMOA
SECRET

The obscure Lā`ie sky reflects
Ka maka hinahina
Misty rain gently falls
On the inviting sand
Ke Ko`olau echoes with whistling winds
Lightning and thunder rumble the land
Ka `ua flows viciously
The pounding nalu hammer
Slams vigorous strikes
The yawning sun
Another day with
Pahumoa.

Kalani Palada

NĀ HUA ʻŌLELO

Māliʻe - calm
Keʻokeʻo - white
Koʻakoʻa - coral
Waianapanapa - caves and beach, Hāna, East
                          Maui
ʻAe - tradewinds
Kanaio - area past Makena, Maui

HŌ`OKAHI NŌ
DEFINITELY NUMBER ONE

Māli`e land
Leans in ocean blue
Ke`okeo sands glow
Beneath the strewn ko`ako`a
Sink your eyes into its depth
The shrouded black sand
Of Waianapanapa
Kisses its edges
The `ae breeze of `Īao caresses Waiehu
The heaves of leaden rain
Spill across Hāna
Darkness falls
With the strong winds of Kanaio
Skyward, a single star still glows.

Aiza Ravida

NĀ HUA ʻŌLELO

Loko - graceful
E - soft command
Manu - bird
Ai luna ʻoe - you are up there
Kukui - light
Makuahine - mother
Keiki - child

KA `A`O LOKO
THE GRACEFUL SHEARWATER

E manu, in the sky
Happy and free
Sweet yet sorrowful
You aloha like no tomorrow
Through good times and bad, ai luna `oe
Oh nurse bird
He kukui through the darkness
Singing along the trails
Leading the lost
You are pushed to death
E makuahine
Your keiki mimic you.

Genita Mae Cabbat

NĀ HUA ʻŌLELO

Kaimana - diamonds
ʻAʻole poina - never forgotten
Ia lā aʻe - day after day
Kiopaʻa - the North Star

NĀ HŌKŪ A ME KA PŌ
THE STARS AND THE NIGHT

The night needs the stars,
As the stars need the night
Ka pō is blunt and boring
Without the heavens light
Nā hōkū glitter like nā kaimana,
Like polished pond pebbles with glory
Sometimes nā hōkū fall from the sky
But soon are forgotten
Without asking why
Only one sun shines always
Deep in the heart of night
`A`ole poina, never lose light
There to guide the way and shine ia lā a`e
Kiopa`a gives ka pō all the light it needs
The night in contrast to the earth can see
The stars need the night,
As the night needs the stars.

Alexis Felicilda

NĀ HUA ʻŌLELO

Naʻenaʻe - daisy
Mana - power
Kumu - teacher

KE KUMU NA`ENA`E
THE DAISY TEACHER

I nestled in a field
And as I sat
I watched a na`ena`e grow
It was barely beyond my touch
But I felt its mana just the same
As the na`na`e grew I also felt
I was kumu too.

Charish Mae Jose

NĀ HULU ʻŌLELO

Nani - pretty
Poepoe - round
Lehua - bottle brush flower
Onaona - alluring
ʻOluʻolu - happy
Ma luna - over
Hualālai. - volcano, Kona, Hawaiʻi Nui
Ulu - breadfruit
Moana - sea
Hoʻonanea - peaceful
Puʻuwai - heart
Ka Mehameha - The lonely one

KA MĀLAMALAMA
O KA MAHINA KONA
CARING KONA MOONLIGHT

Nani kona moon, poepoe in the sky
All is pono
The stars, a sweet kukui celestial lei
In harmony with the monthly orb.
Onaona, `olu`olu ma luna o Hualālai
The silver light glitters on the tasty ulu
The sky shell shines smiles
Over the shimmering moana
Controlling the ho`onanea tides
E kukui o ka pu`uwai
Ka mahina e mauna glow
Over the land of Ka Mehameha.

Jenalyn Paludipan

NĀ HUA ʻŌLELO

Nalu - wave
Hoʻonanea - be at ease
Nana - relaxed
Malino - calm

KA MOANA, KA `INO, KA LĀ
THE SEA, THE STORM, THE SUN

Nalu after nalu
The sea is enraged
Pound away at the forsaken shores
The `ino worsens
Slowly, out comes the sun
Night becomes day
"Shhh...Ho`onanea," cries the sun
Ashamed, the `ino vanishes
Nanea, nana
The sea is malino once again.

Jenissa Olero

NĀ HUA `ŌLELO

Kū - stand
Manakō - mango
`A`ala. - scented
Ke`oke`o `awapuhi - white ginger
Manjito - green Japan bird
Pūpalō - deer
Kanahele - forest
Kahikū - sun between morning and noon

KŪ, E KA PANIANA
STAND, OH BANYAN

Kū ka paniana
Graven and forlorn
Left behind from his manakō companion
`A`ala, by the surrounding
Ka `awapuhi ke`oke`o
Still the manjito flock for a seat
With the pūpalō shaded beneath
Roots running deep
Weathered through many storms
Shielding Ka nahele
And the scalding lā kahikū
Ku, E Ka paniana.

Kelly Rodrigues

NĀ HUA `ŌLELO

Ka Pi`o - the arch
Ma`alae`a - bay, South Maui
Waikapū - area Central Maui
Kaka`ikahi - rarity
Mino`aka - smile
Nā hala Kahiki - pineapples

KA PI`O O KE ĀNUENUE
THE ARCH OF THE RAINBOW

Between Ma`alae`a and Waikapū
Stood he Kaka`ikahi
Breaching at night
Its vibrant colors bursting
The unfading rainbow arch
The bent beauty brings
A mino`aka to my cheeks
A strong sensational delight
To all who witness
I see your arch, I weep
In memory, in celebration
Of the return of the dove
The mountains hear your glow
Nā hala Kahiki share your joy
Let me once again smile.

Jenny Shiffler

NĀ HUA ʻŌLELO

Hoʻoheno - cherished
Konikoni I ka puʻuwai - passion in the heart
Hoʻoipo - loved
Kauʻakau - season after season
Aʻala - scent

KA PUA MAE `OLE
THE NEVER FADING FLOWER

It begins as ho`oheno
A me konikoni I ka pu`uwai
And ends as ho`oipo
Ka Pua has already bloomed
Nā kau akau, I keep it close
The a`ala is forever
My pua mae`oe.

Cherish Sistoza

NĀ HUA ʻŌLELO

Pūkoko - blood red
Koʻu puʻuwai - my heart
Honi - kiss
Kuku - thorn

KA PUA ROSE
THE ROSE

A beauty of a rose
Bold and pūkoko
Enchanted feelings
Run through my veins
Temptation arises
Ko`u pu`uwai beats, thumps
I give it a honi
A touch, a prick
Love so thick
Drips down my finger
A stab from the kuku
Untouchable and lovely
It seeps into my heart
What I seek can never be.

Joy Sohn

NA HUA`ŌLELO

Hekili - thunder
Tsa! - bothersome
Hao - squeaking tree
Waokele - upland forest
Makani ikaika - strong winds
Hele aku - go away
He mea kulikuli - noisy thing

KA MAKIKA
THE MOSQUITO

Sometimes louder than ka hekili I ka Lani
Tsa! Whirring endlessly
Like rubbing hao in the waokele
During nā makani ikaika
E hele aku `oe, he mea kulikuli.

Kiki Souza

The following section presents three poems that are not kaona but are other genre of mele created by Wayne and by early Hawaiians as well. The first is a poem of place, the second a travel poem, and the third a poem recalling a memory.

OTHER POETIC GENRE:
PLACE
TRAVEL
MEMORY

DEDICATED TO
GEORGE ENRIQUES

NĀ HUA ʻŌLELO

Ewa - plain east of Pearl Harbor
Puna - area Southeast Hawaiʻi Nui
Waimea - area North Oʻahu
Nohili - area near Barking Sands, Kauaʻi
ʻŌmaʻomaʻo - cotton
Mauna Kukui - Highest peak of Mauna Eʻeka
ʻĀina hānau - homeland
Ka Puali Nani - foothill area in Wailuku below
                Mauna Kahalawai

KU`U ONE HĀNAU
THE SANDS OF MY BIRTH

Famous are the sands of
Ewa, Puna, Waimea and Nohili
But none like the sand
Of our our beautiful hill home.
Sacred is this sand
Overlooking the `ōma`oma`o plain
Cool in the shade of Mauna Kukui
Firm is this sand
Each grain important
Each dependent on the other
Fine and peaceful is this sand
You sparkle under the blue of sky
And the gold of sun
Thank you, O Creator
For our `āina hānau
Haina mai ana kapuana
Ke One o ka Puali Nani.

The late Edna Ellis heard rumors that her great grand uncle had served in the military. After some digging and historical assistance, it was confirmed, James Bush had served in the navy, but surprise, it was during the American Civil War! This travel mele is about his travels home.

NĀ HUA `ŌLELO

Ka Nene `Aukai - metaphor for ship

Raiatea - Second largest of the Society Islands
In French Polynesia

Pora Pora (Bora Bora) Island group in the Leeward Western Islands of French Polynesia

Tiare - Tahitian gardenia, National flower of French Polynesia and Cook Islands

Papeete - Capital of French Polynesia

Kaho`olawe - Smaller of 8 major Hawaiian Islands - Pathway to Tahiti

Kilohōkū - star gazer

Hōkūle`a (Star of Gladness) - Arcturus, one of the guiding stars for Hawaiian navigators.

`Aina - land

Ko`olau - mountain range, east coast of O`ahu

Noe - fog, mist

Vandalia - USS 18 gun sloop-of-war used to catch blockade runners

Beauregard - Confederate privateer, purchased by Union Navy to block runners

KA NENE `AUKAI O KIMO
JAMES' WHITE SEABIRD

Raiatea's spiked peaks
Were dipping in the distance
The purple silhouette of Pora Pora
Dominated the twilight
The scents of tiare and vanilla
Were fondly dissipating
A brisk wind filled
The imaginary sails of old
The Land under the Clouds finally fades.

It was now open sea, and memories
The navigator has aligned Papeete
With Kaho`olawe
Kilohōkū must wait, anticipating gladness
Bestowed by Hōkūle`a, our `aina's lighthouse.

Reminiscences tumble under him
Like the rolling waves
The Piscatagua River, Sagamore Creek
A hot oyster stew at Florence's
A pint or two at Stoodley's Tavern
Portsmouth's Isle of Schools
Reflecting its' silly names:
(James' White Bird continued on next page)

(White Seabird continued)

Smuttynose, Star, Appledore

He had served, caught up in a war,
The Isles of Bright Sky he left behind
For future peaks - the Crowns of the Ko`olau

The poison of gunpowder
Close quartered coughing
And cold nights on watch
Now plagued his maw immutably
The unseen scars of battle.
His respites in Tahiti and San Francisco
Had eased the pain of war fatigue
His wanderlust, lost

How soothing the Barbary Coast fog
Had been, for awhile
The quiet noe of the Embarcadero
The hills of North Beach
And almost like clockwork
The noon chimes from St. Mary's
Replaced the nagging moody foghorns
Out beyond Fisherman's Wharf
The clearing mists unveiling
Alcatraz, Oakland, and Marin
(White Seabird continued on next page)

(White Seabird continued)

His heart's compass was set
For the Sandwich Isles
To settle,
To find a loving spouse,
To give back, give more

Tonight was quiet, a mum moon
A sedated sea
Much like life on the Vandalia, waiting
Waiting for the blockade runners
Sneaking in the shadows of night
His boys barring supplies to the Grey
At Charleston, Bull's Bay,
Norfolk, and Typee Roads

Back to Portsmouth, a slight reprieve
A new floating home, the Beauregard
This time the southern tip, the Gulf
Tampa, Smyrna, St. Augustine, Key West

How cruel war
There in the distance white sandy coastlines
Taunt the crew and him
The strands rival
The white beaches of Waikīkī
(White Seabird continued on next page)

(White Seabird continued)

How he'd like to float in its' soothing surf
Soak his wounds, refresh his body
Hush his soul
He looks for mountains but there are none
How he misses the mountains

He carved the passing days
On a slab of chestnut
As he incised the last stroke
Of the estimated arrival
Cries of "Diamond Head!" "Diamond Head!"
Seduced crew and passengers to the rails

But Honolulu had changed
He desired more peace
And imagined Kaua`i his birthplace,
his home
Where he would settle
Marry a loving spouse
And share his aloha.

NĀ HUA `ŌLELO
(for opposite page)
Bambucha - pidgin English for big

WAILUKU, 1957

Mom is ironing by the window
It's October, the curtains hardly rustling
I watch the radio
The Pidgin announcer mangles English
Play by play
The palm fronds louver
A fat, Autumn moon.
In a halo under the light pole
The policeman drops his comics
And races to the Dairy Queen
Earlier, some newlyweds
Had gone by, honking
Mama raced to the window
To yell, "Jackass!"

It's October again,
The Fall bambutcha moon
Crowns Haleakalā
Stars still filter
Through the coconut leaves
She's gone now,
But Mama still stands by the window,
Ironing.

I don't write songs;
songs write me.

Sammy Cahn

SONG LYRICS
BY
WAYNE MONIZ

DEDICATED TO
ENGLISH LANGUAGE
CONSULTANT
CHARLOTTE BOTEILHO
&
HAWAIIAN LANGUAGE
CONSULTANT
KALEHUA

-The Makawao 4th of July Rodeo and Parade has been held ever since its founding in 1956 by the Maui Roping Club under the leadership of George Manoa Sr. and Harold "Oskie" Rice.

-Makawao, located on the northwestern slopes of Haleakala at the 1,578 feet level, has been a cowboy town ever since Captain George Vancouver offered a gift of cattle to King Kamehameha the Great In 1793.

-King Kamehameha III later brought Mexican Vaqueros from Vera Cruz to the islands to show the locals the essential skills of tending cattle. Locals first called these Mexican trainers Espaniolo, that, in time, was shortened to Paniolo - a term used today for all cowboys throughout the islands.

NĀ HUA `ŌLELO

(for next two pages)

Oskie Rice -rodeo arena/founder

`Ohana - family

Eddie Tam's - community center/fields named after one of Maui's mayors

Pūlehu pipi - broiled beef

Malasadas - Portuguese sugar donuts

Mālie - calm

`Ōkole - backside

Maika`i - good

THE MAKAWAO 4TH OF JULY PARADE

(CHORUS) Oh, I'm going up to Makawao
To the 4th of July Parade
Oh, I'm going up to Makawao,
I think I've got it made
You pass through Pukalani,
To Oskie Rice you go
Oh, we're going up to Makawao
To the cow and pony show.

Let's do-si-do with Aunty Lu,
Marie, and Rusty too
Uncle Ed and John and Stan
And Uncle Stephen do.
Oh, listen good to Uncle Butch,
Hear him make the call
And promenade with Makaleka
All around the hall.

Oh, I like to ride up on a float
In the 4th of July Parade
I wave aloha to `ohana
In the mango shade

(4th of July continued on next page)

We're heading up to Eddie Tam's
For good ole country fun
I've got my boot, ten gallon hat
For the smiling Maui sun.
(Repeat Chorus)

Oh, I can smell pulehu pipi
Sizzlin on the grills
Bean soup and malasadas,
They give me ono trills
And underneath one real big tent,
The band begins to play
And in the background scene,
Mālie Kahului Bay.

When summer comes, you know it's time
To join the jamboree
The slopes of Haleakalā is
Where you want to be.
Get your `ōkole up the slope,
Mary, John, let's go
Don't miss the Makawao Parade's
Maika`i rodeo.
(Repeat Chorus)

ORIGINAL SONG FROM HIBISCUS POMADE -THE MUSICAL OF THE SAME NAME- BY WAYNE MONIZ

Hibiscus Pomade, the musical, is my Hawaiian version of "Grease" with a salute in the title song to The Four Seasons. In Hawai`i, the grease came in jars in several floral varieties (hibiscus, pikake, etc.) that kept our hair straighter in this humid clime. They were a lot thicker and pity the poor fly that landed on it - he'd never get away. "Hibiscus Pomade" was the theme song of my 60s musical by the same name. (2002)

HIBISCUS POMADE

(Intro)

Doo wop doo wop doo wap doo wah ah
Doo wop doo wop doo wap wah ah

(CHORUS) Hibiscus Pomade
You're the one I adore
Hibiscus Pomade
I always want more
Hibiscus Pomade
You brought my baby to me
Doo wop doo wah ah.

Hibiscus Pomade
Let that Maui moon shine
Down on my crown
And I know she'll be mine
Hibiscus Pomade
You drew my lover to me
Doo wop doo wah ah

(Hibiscus Pomade continued
on next page.)

(Hibiscus Pomade cont.)

You know I tried gardenia
Pikake, tuberose
But you, my fair hibiscus
You're the sweetest flower that grow oh oh ohs.

Hibiscus Pomade
I love your soft goo
Hibiscus Pomade
Tres Flores won't do
Hibiscus Pomade
You sent an angel to me.

(Repeat Chorus

Hibiscus Pomade
It's not greasy kid's stuff
Hibiscus Pomade
I can't get enough
Hibiscus Pomade
Brilliantine just won't do
("Walk Like a Man" ending)
Doo oo oo oo oo oo oo oo (drum beat)

ORIGINAL SONGS FROM STILL BORN: NĀ MELE O KAHO`OLAWE A PLAY BY WAYNE MONIZ

On January 17, 1893, a group of foreigners staged a coup d'état against the Hawaiian government.

UĒ KĀKOU I KĒIA PŌ
WE CRY TONIGHT

We cry tonight
They snuffed out our light
They steal our dignity.

We cry tonight
They do un-right
Make mad our sanity.

We cry tonight
They blind our sight
They damn our clarity.

We cry tonight
We try to fight
With no majority.

What did the Woman do
That they treat her mean that way?
What did our good Queen do
That they've taken her away.

She's gone - our all
Our kingdom's fall
That's why
We cry tonight.

-On January 6, 1976 a group of more than 50 Hawaiians attempted an invasion of the island of Kaho`olawe; They would eventually become Protect Kaho`olawe `Ohana (PKO). The protest spurred on a revival of Hawaiian activism.

-In 1993, the island was returned to the State of Hawai`i. The State Legislature created the Kaho`olawe Hawaiian Reserve. Members and friends of the Protect Kaho`olawe `Ohana were allowed back on the island for cleanup as well as for cultural and religious practices.

MA KĒLĀ `AO`AO KE ALA
ACROSS THE WAY

Across the way, the lights I see
From darkness on my side
Maui's shape, outlined in neon
Bright lights upon her tide.

Chorus:
Rush on, oh rushing ocean
Rush on, oh precious foam
Be constant, tides returning
The sea, my love, my home.

My island longs for loving
She cries in servile state
Her captors slight her power
They ignore her forc`ed fate.

When she's tired of desecration
The sea reclaims her own
Same the land in restoration
Re-takes each sacred stone.

(Chorus)

On the night prior to the January 6, 1976 invasion of Kaho`olawe, two of the protestors, George Helm and Kimo Mitchell set out on surfboards to Kanaloa Kohemālamalama. They were never heard from again.

HE LA`A KEA I HELE KĀUA
THERE'S A BRIGHT LIGHT
THAT WE GO TO

There's a bright light that we go to
Far across the sea
It's a peaceful place to paddle to
A land of harmony.

There's a bright light that we go to
Where our ancestors went before
Its tranquil vale to stroll through
Where full aloha is in store.

There's a bright light that we go to
Moonbeams set the way
A mission that's ongoing
Through every lasting day.

There's a bright light that we go to
The Face of Truth we'll see
We love staring in the Eyes of God
Our lives' true Destiny.

NA MELE O KAHO`OLAWE
by Uncle Harry Kunihi Mitchell

You are the southern beacon
Barren and without population
Until you were invaded
By nine young men
Who granted you peace.

Let us band together
The Hawaiian Kingdom
From sun up to sun down
Stand together and follow
Be strong, young people
We are but a few in numbers
But our love of the land is unlimited.

Popular are the young people
Of Hawai`i Nei
For the civil strife
They cause against the government
Together in one thought
To bring prosperity to the land
Forward young people
And bring salvation
To Kaho`olawe.

NĀ MELE KAUMAHA
O KA MAHINA MAUI
MAUI MOON BLUES

I'm feeling low
The moon responds so
I'm feeling blue
He feels that way too.

(Chorus) I guess you can tell
I'm feeling like hell
But someday I'll lose
Those Maui Moon Blues.

The Man in the Moon
He usually smiles
But he's wearing a frown
And I'm feeling down.

Oh, sometimes I'm up
And sometimes I'm down
Like that ole chunk-o-cheese
I'm ill, not at ease.

(Chorus)

(Maui Moon Blues continued on next page)

(Maui Moon Blues cont.)

When I'm down on my luck
To the heavens I scan
I look for a friend
For my problems to end.

One has left me before
For a more perfect mate
But rather than die
I look up to the sky.

(Chorus)

HAU PE`E PE`E
HIDE AND SEEK

This game is just a mockery
We imitate the old
Who run and play their hide and seek
And ruin other people's souls,

Like ring-around-the-rosey
A dirge, bubonic curse
They use the game of cat and mouse
To make conditions worse.

It's a deadly game of fox and hounds
That try our brothers' souls
Unlike the children in the yard
Whose games have faultless goals.

Ready or not, here they come!
They did not count to ten
They break the rules they don't like
Not children, more like men.

They kick the can and steal the flag
And cover up the base

(Hide and Seek continued on next page)

(Hide and Seek continued)

Unlike the children they once were
Their behavior's a disgrace.

Quit harmful games and tell no lies
like the guileless play with glee
Let our adult diversions
Reflect youth's harmony.

HE MELE HOENA HAWAI`I
A HAWAIIAN PADDLING SONG

Let's paddle all the islands
Sail to all the eight
Hail aloha to our `aina
Praise our islands great.

Catch the swells to Ni`ihau
Pearly shells sing of the sea
Angelic voices raised
Forerunners planted seeds.

The current moves us to Kaua`i
The rugged peaks near Hanalei
Caves and canyons full of awe
Mokihana branches sway.

Stroke quickly to O`ahu's sands
Challenge surfers to the shore
Imposing Mount Le`ahi
Where duck ponds are no more.

(Paddling Song continued on next page)

(Paddling song cont.)

Next on to fair Lāna`i
The red dirt that's our land
The Norfolk whisper wind tales
Lāna`i extends a hand.

Ho`omau! Kaho`olawe
Held captive and in pain
Your beauty hostage hidden
You shall be free again.

The scent of sweet Lokelani
Maui breezes call to me
The giant Haleakalā
Shades Hāna by the sea.

Down the chain - Hawai`i Nui
Kīlauea's great expanse
Mauna Kea, Mauna Loa
Spewed by Pele's trance.

We paddled through the islands
We see jewels the gods have dropped
May these same gods still protect her
May aloha never stop.

HAPA HAOLE SONG CIRCA 1941

So lets...
Sing a silly song
That paints Hawai`i wrong
Let's write a silly rhyme
And get away with crime.

Let's say Hawaiians play
Like beach boys every day
We'll pretend they always smile
And can surf a good long mile.

Girls shake their hula skirts
Those fair young maidens flirt
Come strum a hapa haole tune
Under a hapa haole moon.

Let Bob and Bing sing a swing
With monkeys who don't live here
These movies showed just what's sarong
Lamours are what we fear.

(Hapa Haole Song continued on next page)

(Hapa Haole Song continued)

Let's make the isles a U.S. State
Manifest destiny is our fate
Let's sway those shiny cellophanes
And mangle simple Hawaiian names.

What we sang is partly true
But only half, no shaded hue
There's much more to what we are
A real Hawaiian is the star.

So let's...
Sing a silly song
That paints Hawai`i wrong
Let's write a silly rhyme
And get away with Crime.

-BONUS-
A NEW PLAY
BY
WAYNE MONIZ

From
Roselani Blossom
By
Johnny Almeida

`Auhea wale ana `oe
E ka liko pua lokelani
He nani nui `oe na`u
No nā kau a kau.

Where could you be
O bud of the lokelani blossom
You are a heavenly being for me
Now and forever.

Kau nui aku ka mana`o
I ka wai a`o `Īao
Ua inu au a kena
I ka `ono a`o ia wai.

One's thoughts are always drawn
To the waters of `Īao
I have slaked my thirst
On that sweet water.

`ĪAO:
KAHI MĀKOU E HELE AI
MA NĀ ĀNUENUE

`ĪAO
WHERE WE WALK THROUGH
RAINBOWS
©2022

A Poetic Drama

INTRODUCTION

I was walking through ʻĪao Valley
several years back when a
rainbow appeared near me.
It was so close that I decided
to walk through it.
It was a once in a lifetime experience.
The Valley inspired me to tell its tale.

PRODUCTION NOTES

This play is originally written
as an outdoor "moving play";
acts take place in different areas
on the venue property.
Of course, there is the option to do
the production indoors in one setting.
The script does not contain any *oli* or hula
but the intent of the playwright
was to insert appropriate oli
or hula in particular scenes
as well as at the beginning and end.
The director should work
with recommendations of
kumu hula/advisor.

SYNOPSIS OF SCENES

ACT ONE
Hawai`i Loa's
Double Hulled Canoe.

ACT TWO, SCENE ONE
Outside the Hale of Maui and Hina,
`Īao Valley.

ACT THREE
Compound of King Olepau.
`Īao Valley.

ACT THREE, SCENE TWO
The Road Past Kahakuloa.

ACT FOUR
Wailuku Campsite
of
Kamehameha Nui.

ACT FIVE
The Veranda of the Maui Hotel.
Wailuku.

ACT SIX
Sheriff's Command Post.
Wailuku School.

CAST OF CHARACTERS

ACT ONE

`Iao - The Steersman - Narrator
Hawai`i Loa - Chief Navigator
Hualalai - Hawai`i Loa's Wife
O`ahu a Lua - Their Daughter
Maui - Their First Born Son
Kaua`i - Their Youngest Son
Wai`ale`ale - Kaua`i's Wife
Makali`i - Steersman
Child
Dog

ACT TWO

`Iao, The Daughter of Maui and Hina
Maui
Hina
Pu`uokamoa - The Merman

ACT THREE
SCENE ONE

Hi`iaka - Younger Sister of Pele
Wahine `Ōma`o - half goddess/
Hi`iaka's Fellow Traveler
Pa`uopala`e - Hi`iaka's Nurse
Kuakahimahiku - Kahuna

ACT THREE
SCENE TWO

Kuakahimahiku
First Koa
Second Koa
Hi`iaka
Wahine `Ōma`o
Child
Dog

ACT FOUR

Kamehameha Nui
Holo`ae - His Battle Kahuna

ACT FIVE

Mark Twain
Reporter #1
Reporter #2

ACT SIX

Deputy Sheriff Mahi
Sheriff Crowell

EPILOGUE

ACT ONE

THE DOUBLE HULLED CANOE
OF HAWAI`I LOA.
NIGHT.

(`Īao is at the helm.
The sound of wind and waves.
There are occasional sounds coming
from pigs, chickens, and dogs.
Hawai`i Loa is heard from offstage.)

VOICE
(of Hawai`i Loa)
The wind strapped us harshly
For awhile there.
Are we still on course?

`ĪAO
(yelling back)
We are on course.

HAWAI`I LOA
(entering)
You've guided us well, cousin.
We're getting close and thanks to you,
We're arriving safely. You deserve
an *inoa kapakapa* for guiding us well.
Can you think of what that name might be?

ʻĪAO

I don't know but I do know that I owe it all
To that great bright light - ʻĪao.

HAWAIʻI LOA

A good choice - the light that doesn't blink...

ʻĪAO

...The *Kukui* that burns on all night...
E, but I don't know if it fits.

HAWAIʻI LOA

A new name is like new *kapa*...too stiff...
Needs to be worn to comfort.

ʻĪAO

True. I would be most thankful
For a name like ʻĪao.

HAWAIʻI LOA

Without you, like
Without that moving star,
We would be wandering aimlessly.
Your skill has made us secure.

ʻĪAO

Mahalo, e Hawaiʻi Loa.
But I cannot take the thanks alone.
All the other oarsmen
And steersmen are skillful.

HAWAI`I LOA
True.

`IAO

To add to your confidence,
I feel land is near
We've seen more *manu* and
Drifting leaves and branches.

HAWAI`I LOA

I'll be back shortly. Stay the course, `Iao,
Stay the course.

`IAO

*Ho`okele* `Iao. Mmm. It has a nice sound.
The predictions of Makali`i and me
Have been proven right.
We've silenced the nay-sayers.
You'll drown…be eaten by monsters…
You'll drift aimlessly without water.
(He turns to the audience as Narrator)
My predictions came in dreams
As I stood here
Night upon night.
I could envision this place.
We'd name it Hawai`i after our great father
Who brought us here.

We would successfully find these islands
Unoccupied, unchartered.
As seafaring people,
We've seen all kinds
Of islands, simple rocks
Plunging downward
Windswept cliffs with little life,
Uninhabitable lands
Of blackened desolation...
But these are in my dreams...
These have beauty like no others.
Its precious flowers are its valleys
And one of the most beautiful is ʻĪao.
You've come here on my watch
And so I'll continue my job as navigator
Not as a navigator of the seas
But as a navigator through life;
Not the life of a human being but of a valley
The life of a valley filled with humanity.
In this vision that I unfold before you.
I'll use the help of the
Travelers on this canoe
To unveil the story of ʻĪao Valley.
(The players are announced then exit into
darkness.)

ĪAO
(announcing)
Hawai`i Loa
Hualalai - His wife
Maui - Their first born son
O`ahu a Lua - Their daughter
Kaua`i - Their youngest son
Wai`ale`ale - His wife
Makali`i - his chief steersman.
A Child
A Dog

Remember,`Īao is not only my name
But it also happens to be the name of the
Daughter of Maui and Hina.
Our life of `Īao Valley starts
With the story of that daughter.
Let's follow her
As she has been summoned by her *makua*.
(`Īao the navigator, grabs a torch.
He is joined by `Īao,
The daughter of Maui and Hina.
She holds a calabash.
He asks the audience to follow him.)
Come join me, people. Let's go with `Īao
To see her father, Maui
And her mother, Hina
(Along the way, `Īao,
the Daughter of Maui, speaks.)

`ĪAO THE DAUGHTER
I'm afraid to talk to my mother and father.

`ĪAO THE NAVIGATOR
Why is that?

`ĪAO THE DAUGHTER
A helper at the compound told me
They look angry.

`ĪAO THE NAVIGATOR
Why? Have you done anything
To upset them?

`ĪAO THE DAUGHTER
Well...
(They approach the *hale*.)

ACT TWO

OUTSIDE THE *HALE'* OF THE DEMIGOD MAUI AND HINA. `ĪAO VALLEY. NIGHT.

Hina pounds *kapa*,
Maui works on a fishhook.
The pounding stops
as their daughter approaches.
The silence is pervasive.

`ĪAO
Aloha, *e makuakane, makuahine*.
(There is no response.)
No response. What? No aloha tonight?

MAUI
Where have you been, daughter?

`ĪAO
Gathering *ukiuki* berries as I said I would.

HINA
And you saw no one in the *maukele*?

`ĪAO
No one in the forest except
the *manu* chirping endlessly.

MAUI
What about Pu`uokamoa?

`ĪAO
(caught but covering)
Oh, I forgot. I passed him
on his way to fetch *o`opu*…

HINA
A human *manu* chirps differently…

`ĪAO
A human *manu*?

MAUI
He said he saw you
With Puuokamoa, the Merman,
Along the stream.

`ĪAO
I have to pass that way
To pick the *ukiuki* berries.
I can't avoid it to do my duties.

HINA
We will warn him not to be there
When you pass.

`ĪAO
(softly)
`Ae.

MAUI
You will not keep company with him.
You are *kapu*
From all until I tell you
What (emphasizing) man
Will be your lover.

HINA
We must leave now, Maui

MAUI
We are meeting with your uncles tonight
And must go.
You tend to your duties.

(They leave.
ʻĪao lights two *kukui* lamps by the *puka*.
She also puts some food into a gourd
and heads out. The audience and Navigator
follow ʻĪao, The Daughter.)

ALONG THE ʻĪAO STREAM. NIGHT.

(Puʻuokamoa is waiting in the dark
as ʻĪao the Daughter enters.)

PUʻUOKAMOA
I saw the two lit *kukui* from your *puka*
And hurried here.

ʻĪAO
Father and mother were angry with me.
We were spied on earlier.

PUʻUOKAMOA
Did anyone see you as you came here?

ʻĪAO
I looked well. No one did.

PU`UOKAMOA
I thought someone was behind you
As you approached.

`ĪAO
You're worried again, Pu`uokamoa.

PU`UOKAMOA
How can I not be worried
After you told me about the *kapu*,
Then this…

`ĪAO
It's a natural *kapu*.
No father wants to see his daughter
Carried away
By the first male that comes along.

PU`UOKAMOA
But you're no common girl.
You are the daughter of a demigod.

`ĪAO
What is he saving me for?
(changing the subject)
Enough of this nonsense.
I've missed you, Pu`uokamoa,
Since you've been away.

PU`UOKAMOA
It's only been hours…

`ĪAO
…A day…a year. Oh, Pu`uokamoa,
We can't always
Meet under these conditions -
Always hiding,
Always holding back in formal greetings.
Let's escape from this place.

PU`UOKAMOA
And make it worse!
Maui will track me down and kill me.
Perhaps we need to be patient.
When your reach womanhood
Then your purpose will change.

`ĪAO
I'm a *wahine* already, Pu`uokamoa.
Or don't you believe it?

PU`UOKAMOA
Oh, I can't deny that…
And a beautiful one.
(They kiss;
Suddenly Pu`uokamoa is startled.)
Who was that?

`ĪAO
Pu`uokamoa? Again?

PU`UOKAMOA
No, `Īao. It was someone.
I saw the flip of a *malo*;
He was hiding in the *awapuhi*.
Perhaps we'd better leave.

`ĪAO
No, Pu`uokamoa…
the night is still young.
Father and Mother are gone.
Stay until I must go.

PU`UOKAMOA
Why is it that the best is always *kapu*?
(They kiss again.)

`ĪAO
We must make new plans
As to where we meet.
Father says that you must not be
Where I walk.

PU`UOKAMOA
Then I need to leave the island…

`ĪAO
…then I'll go with you.

PU`UOKAMOA
You can't!

`IAO
(embracing him)
I love you too much, Puuokamoa.
We must go. (She kisses him.
A noise is heard.)

PU`UOKAMOA
Shh. Someone's in the forest.

MAUI
(emerging with Hina in the dark)
It's just another human *manu*…

`IAO
…Father?!

MAUI
Daughter? Liar? Breaker of *kapu*?

PU`UOKAMOA
My Lord, Maui, It was I who…

MAUI
Excuses are past. Your words told me
All I need to know
Do you realize the consequences?

`ĪAO
Father, surely you're not going to…

MAUI
(loudly and angrily)
Wasn't the *kapu* spoken to you clearly?
I never knew my daughter was deaf.

`ĪAO
Father, I plead, spare him.

MAUI
And make my laws a laugh. Stupid Maui!
He makes laws that anyone can disobey.
What an old fool!

PU`UOKAMOA
You're no fool, oh famous Maui.

MAUI
But you are…

`ĪAO
(pleading)
Didn't Maui once break a *kapu*?
Be honest, Father,
Should death be a punishment
For loving?
(no response)

(ʻĪao continued)
Father, I cannot live
Without the sight of Puuokamoa.
His beauty is irresistible to me.
He calms me, awes me,
Inspires me. And Father,
This failure was not meant
To harm you.
I was simply following my heart.
You said that
I should do that
When we talked about aloha. You said
That aloha was especially important
When a man was feeling low.
Father, I beg you, show some mercy.

MAUI
(intensely)
Kapu is *kapu*!
However, you did say a few words
That may be a way
To appease both you and our gods.

ʻĪAO
(confused)
What was that, *Makuakane*?

MAUI
You cannot live without the sight of him?
I have a solution. Choose either death
Or your desire to see him forever.

`ĪAO
There is no choice except the last one.

MAUI
Then go now, Pu`uokamoa.
Climb to the top of the innermost mouth
Of this ancient volcano.
And you, Daughter, your wish
Will be granted. In the morning,
From the *puka* of our Hale,
Look *ma luna*
And you'll see Pu`uokamoa
Always
There - a glorious pinnacle of stone
Set against a blue sky
And white clouds.

(`Īao weeps. The couple kisses
for the last time and
Pu`uokamoa leaves
as the scene fades to black.)

`ĪAO THE NAVIGATOR
(narrating)
A cruel way to appease a daughter?
Perhaps.
However, future generations
Are the inheritors of
Maui's heartbreaking decision.
They too, like many
Visitors to the valley,

Now gaze like `Īao did at the
Handsome 1, 200 foot
Perpetual monument
To her lover, the Merman, Pu`uokamoa.

Shortly after Maui had dragged the Islands
Up from the sea, and after the story of
`Īao and Pu`uokamoa,
Some new travelers
made Hawai`i their destination -
They were
The Pele Clan.
They had come to the islands
In search of fire,
Proceeding as if on stepping stones
Down the island chain.
After Lehua and Ni`ihau
They stopped off on Kaua`i.
It was there that Lohi`au
Caught the eye of Pele.
The clan continued down the chain
With Lohi`au
Deep in the heart of Pele.
When she reached Hawai`i Nui
And settled in a her home
at Halema`uma`u,
She called forward her favorite sister.
'Hi`iaka," she told her,
Return to Kaua`i
And bring Lohi`au back to Kīlauea.'

Hi`iaka set forth on her journey
with two companions,
Wahine Oma`o and Pa`uopala`e.
Pele and Hi`iaka both believed
That their reputation as goddesses
Would proceed them
And be reason enough
To afford Hi`iaka
And her two companions,
The same hospitality
Any human being
Should have been awarded.
Let us join Hi`iaka,

ACT THREE
SCENE ONE

THE GROUNDS
BEFORE THE COMPOUND
OF THE MAUI ALI`I `OLEPAU. `
IAO VALLEY. EVENING.

(Wahine Oma`o and Pa`uopala`e
Have approached `Iao Valley.
They had arrived at Kahului
And walked the distance from the bay.
Exhausted, they drop
Their traveling bundles
To the ground.)

WAHINE OMA`O
Hoo. I'm tired and thirsty.

HI`IAKA
We're finally here to greet Ali`i `Olepau
With our hearts open
And our tongues thirsty.

PA`UOPALA`E
Let's not wait for an offer.
Let's run down to the stream.
I can hear it rushing from here.

WAHINE OMA`O
(screaming)
What was that?

PA`UOPALA`E
That's your mind playing games
From trudging across
Those sand dunes.

HI`IAKA
No, she's seeing things, Pa`uopala`e.
I saw it too
Along the far side of my vision.

PA`UOPALA`E
(screaming too)
Oh, there it is. What is it?

HI'IAKA
It fits the description of
Ali'i 'Olepau himself.

WAHINE OMA'O
I've never seen it myself
But I have heard about the
Second soul that leaves the body
Before the first soul
Finally does.

HI'IAKA
That's true, Wahine Oma'o.
He must be near death.

KUAKAHIMAHIKU
(Entering, speaking harshly)
What are you doing in this valley?

HI'IAKA
Aloha too. My name is Hi'iaka...

KUAKAHIMAHIKU
Too many mothers are naming
Their offspring after
Gods and goddesses.
Who are these women?

HI'IAKA
These are my traveling companions.
This is Pa'uopala'e...

WAHINE OMA`O
And I am Wahine Oma`o of Puna.

KUAKAHIMAHIKU
So why are you here?

HI`IAKA
To meet with Ali`i `Olepau
And ask if we can
Be refreshed
And spend the night in the serenity
Of this beautiful valley.

KUAKAHIMAHIKU
Oh, I'm afraid that can't be done…

HI`IAKA
Why?

KUAKAHIMAHIKU
I'm afraid he's asleep.

HI`IAKA
Could he be awakened?
It's almost evening.
I'm sure he's ready
For his evening meal.

KUAKAHIMAHIKU
I am not to awaken him for any reason.

WAHINE OMA`O
What if it concerns his health?

KUAKAHIMAHIKU
What about his health?
Do you know something I don't know?
I don't think so.

PA`UOPALA`E
Could you check on him.
We just saw his ghost and…
(She is kicked by Hi`iaka.)

KUAKAHIMAHIKU
Oh, his ghost? Now I definitely know that
You are evil visitors. Leave the valley now!

HI`IAKA
Sister, we came with good intent.
I am not named after Hi`iaka.
I am Hi`iaka
And we're traveling
Through Maui to go to Kaua`i
Where we will get Lohi`au
And take him back
To our dear sister, Pele.

KUAKAHIMAHIKU
Mo`olelo maker.
A wonderful children's tale.

HI`IAKA

Then don't treat us like gods
But as simple folks, thirsty and tired.
Don't our gods tell us to give aloha?

KUAKAHIMAHIKU

`Olepau has forbidden everyone
From entering the valley. It is his!
And let me add this,
He trusts no gods but his.

HI`IAKA

This vomiter of `Olepau
Speaks blasphemy.
(Hi`iaka grabs her
and yells to Pa`uopala`e.)
Here, grab her Pa`uopala`e!
Tie her with this!
(She throws a woven bag
and shoves it over Kuakahimahiku's head.)
Wahine Oma`o, come with me.
We'll grab the rotten bones
And dying spirit of `Olepau
And take him from this sacred valley.
We'll toss his bones
In the Waihe`e Stream
At our first stop there;
His white shroud will be embedded
Along its banks for all to see -
The day the gods were defiled.

WAHINE OMA`O
At Waihe`e?

HI`IAKA
We'll cast his body on the cliffs
Near the mouth of the river.
(They rush off to get the body.
Pa`uopala`e struggles with Kuakahimahiku.)

PA`UOPALA`E
Stop wiggling, you old crab.
Your selfish ali`i
Has gone his way to the netherworld
Where you should go too.

KUAKAHIMAHIKU
(screaming through the bag)
If you don't release me,
I will make sure that your very flesh
Will be stripped away
And thrown to the dogs.

PA`UOPALA`E
You are the evil one
Who has rejected a goddess
And you will pay for it.

(Hi`iaka and Wahine Oma`o
enter with the remains
of the body in a *kapa* shroud.)

WAHINE OMA`O
He was just skin and bones.
He obviously had wasted away
While this old hag followed his words
Without aloha.

HI`IAKA
Now get down on your knees
Old woman.
And stay until we are gone.
Tell all that they can now go to
Waihe`e to see `Olepau!

PA`UOPALA`E
(getting nervous)
Shh. I faintly see someone
Approaching in the distance!
Let's leave now, quickly.
(They grab their belongings.)
They will hear of the *alii*'s death
And blame it on us.

HI`IAKA
Not if they don't recognize us…

WAHINE OMA`O
Huh?

PA`UOPALA`E
All these gods talk in riddles…

HIʻIAKA
You will see… (They run off.)

KUAKAHIMAHIKU
(struggling, getting free, and yelling)
Help! *Nā Koa!* Help! (The guards rush in.)
Three women have slain the king!
'You!' (to One *koa)*
'Send a group of men
To block off Kahului;
They will not leave that way.
The women are headed to Waiheʻe,
Then Kahakuloa,
Probably to Pōhaku Kāʻanapali,
Where they'll sail to Molokaʻi.
You! (to the other *koa)*
'Gather a group. We'll get ahead of them.
They don't know the island well.
We'll take the mountain trail
And meet them on the road
At Kahakuloa.' (They run off.)

ʻĪAO THE NAVIGATOR
(narrating to the audience)
Come. Let us go
Where Kuakahimahiku intends
To snag Hiʻiaka,
Wahine Omaʻo, and Paʻuopalaʻe.
Several hours have passed.

(ʻĪao the Navigator and the audience
Move to a new scene:
Along the road to Kahakuloa.
Kuakahimahiku is waiting there
With two *koa* with spears.)

ACT THREE
SCENE TWO

KUAKAHIMAHIKU
Poor Hiʻiaka imitator.
Our shortcut gives us a chance
To capture them ourselves.
What a surprise it will be.
I spied movement in the last gully.
They should be here about now.

FIRST KOA
I hear voices.

KUAKAHIMAHIKU
The birds are coming to the trap.
Prepare to snare them.

(An old woman
with a child and a dog enter.)

SECOND KOA
It's not them. It's an old woman
And a child with a dog. (He laughs.)

KUAKAHIMAHIKU
(Confused, embarrassed,
Peering back at the previous valley)
Perhaps they are still on their way.
(To the old woman) '*E Luahine*,
Have you crossed paths
With three women today?'

HI'IAKA
(disguised as the old woman)
We heard from a fisherman
Off to trade his *ʻopihi* in Wailuku
That he spoke to them.
They were headed
To Waiehu Beach.
Perhaps if you hurry back you'll
be able to catch up with them.

KUAKAHIMAHIKU
Hō'ino wale! They deceived us!
(They run off in the opposite direction,)

WAHINE OMAʻO/THE CHILD
(laughing)
E Paʻuopalaʻe, did you know
That you make a fine dog?

HI'IAKA/OLD WOMAN
(laughing)
And you, Wahine Omaʻo.
I've never seen you younger.

WAHINE OMA`O/THE CHILD
Mahalo, e grandmother. (They all laugh.)

HI`IAKA
Well, let's move on, transformed ones,
On to Moloka`i!
(They leave as scene turns to black.)

ĪAO THE NAVIGATOR
(narrating)
`Īao Valley slowly gained its' reputation
As the burial place of *Nā Moî*,
The great *Ali`i Nui* of Hawai`i,
Excluding desecrators like `Olepau.
It would not, however,
Be the burial site of the most
Famous *ali`i* of Hawai`i -
Kamehameha The Great.
His bones would be hidden
On Hawai`i *Nui*
In the enigmatic
Seventh of the Seven Islands.
But `Īao Valley would play
A major role in the
In unification of the islands
By The Lonely One.
Humiliated by his first attempt
To capture Maui, to unify
Under the leadership of Kalaniopu`u,
Kamehameha returned -
A second time to Maui -

Committed to success - in his words
'To Drink of the ʻĪao River.'
This time he had *Lopaka* with him -
Robert,
The named canon
Of a captured foreign ship.
For Kamehameha the time was right.
Kahekili, The fierce *aliʻi nui* of Maui
Was off on Oʻahu
Trying to conquer that island.
Kalanikapule, his son,
was temporarily in charge of the island.
But Kalanikupule was no Kahekili.
He lacked the ruthlessness
Of his father.
This time not only did
Kamehameha
Station an obvious flank
at Māʻalaea
But the bulk of thousands of warriors
Would land at Kahului and Waiehu
and pin Kalanikapule and his Warriors
with their backs to The Wall -
the over thousand foot
Mauna ʻEʻeka
at the rear of ʻĪao River.
Let's go back to that time.

Let's follow Holoʻae,
Kamehameha's *kahuna,*
to Kamehameha's campground.

ACT FOUR

KAMEHAMEHA'S ENCAMPMENT.
WAILUKU. NIGHT.

HOLO`AE
E Pai`ea, O Ali`i Nui.
You wanted to see me?

KAMEHAMEHA
Mahalo, e Holo`ae.
Any good omens yet?

HOLO`AE
Well…?

KAMEHAMEHA
E, Kahuna, why are you holding back?

HOLO`AE
I…the whole battle was played out
in dreams last night…

KAMEHAMEHA
Holo`ae, was it a victory?

HOLO`AE
I can't…

KAMEHAMEHA
Tell me…what's going to happen?

HOLO`AE

You know that I cannot give details,
the sanctity would be broken
and the prediction can change
To our disadvantage.

KAMEHAMEHA

So it was good?
Anyway you told me previously
That you saw visions
Of a plot to kill me
You said I should not, this time,
Go into battle directly
But command from here.
I want to live the battle
Of victory that I cannot experience.
I want to be there
Among my warriors.
It's the only way I can as predicted
Drink of the `Īao.

HOLO`AE

But my *Ali`i*…

KAMEHAMEHA

Kahuna, I insist you tell.
You certainly know me by now.
I will watch my words.
No one will know.
Tell me, now,
Starting from the morning.

HOLO`AE
(putting himself into a trance,
he recites mystically)
Everything you wished.
They flee sadly,
Leaving the second level leaders
To be slaughtered.
The Maui ali`i and Keōpūalani
Scale the narrow exit
At the end of `Īao Valley,
Climb up the rarely trod trails
And come out at Olowalu.
They sail,
The men to O`ahu,
The women to Moloka`i.

KAMEHAMEHA
Running home to father…
And on the second day?

HOLO`AE
Even more glorious than the first.
Kekuhaupi`o leads the charge.
The barbed spears
And stone clubs
Come out.
Kekuhaupi`o lifted many,
Breaking their backs
Upon his knees of stone.

KAMEHAMEHA
And *Lopaka*?
How was our big mouthed friend?

HOLO`AE
Brought in on the third day,
As you commanded.
It was used to perfection.
The canon was placed,
As you apprised us at Kawelowelo,
Aimed up the valley.
The thundering sound
Caused absolute terror
Among the Maui Warriors.
The retreated until
They found themselves
Clawing up the steep cliffs
All the way back of the caldera.
Your advancing army
grabbed at their heels
And dragged
The squealing adversaries
Down to the the river's edge
Onto the massive basalt boulders.
The slashed bodies
were thrown into the `Īao
The corpses clogging up
the once-brawling stream.

KAMEHAMEHA
Mahalo, Holo`ae, my good priest.

HOLO`AE
Enough of visions.
Our supper
Before tomorrow's battle is ready.
Let's go.
(They exit. Fade to black.)

`IAO THE NAVIGATOR
(narrating)
And so the great conquerer
Went on to fulfill the
Visions of his kahuna.
The invasion fleet
Then moved on to O`ahu
And the battle for these islands
Moved to another sacred valley -
Nu`uanu.
After the sensible Kaumuali`i of Kaua`i
Agreed to peaceful unification
The islands finally became one.
The once bloody valley of `Iao
Would return to
Tranquility once again.
A hundred years passed.
The islands were now
Bracing for the turning tide -

The imperialistic clutches
of Europe and the United States.
There were some Americans
Who were offended
By the power grabbers of
Manifest Destiny.
Samuel Clemens,
Of *Huckleberry Finn* fame,
Set out on a voyage to Hawai`i,
And the rest of the World,
To see for himself.
Here come
Some reporters from the
Honolulu Commercial Advertiser.
They're headed over to the *Maui Hotel*
To hear what Mr. Clemens,
Also known as Mark Twain,
Has to say about Hawai`i so far
And his current trip
up to `Īao Valley.

ACT FIVE

THE VERANDA OF THE *MAUI HOTEL*.
AFTER SUPPER.

TWAIN
(patting his stomach)
I think I'm going to settle

(Twain cont.)
Permanently in this hotel
So I can eat more of Mrs. Texeira's
Great Portuguese bean soup.
(He lights his pipe.)
What a night, eh gentlemen?
(They both nod responding yesses.)
Ah, you're spoiled. It's almost like this
Every night. (pointing eastward)
Look over at Haleakalā;
She's aglow now,
Golden from the setting sun.

REPORTER #1
Mr. Twain, are you enjoying
Your trip through the islands?

TWAIN
Hāna, Lahaina, and
(pointing to Haleakalā)
To the top of that grand lady.

REPORTER #2
What you do today?

TWAIN
Well, you can call today,
A day of indolent luxury.
I went with some friends on a picnic
Up the beautiful gorge here.

(Twain cont.)
Have you been up the valley?
(No hands go up.)
What? Oh well, I know some folks
In Missouri that have never
Slapped their feet
On the Mississippi Mud.
Anyway, the trail runs along
The edge of a spirited stream
At the bottom of the canyon.
The horses and riders
Remained cool
Considering it was a hot day.
Massive green canopies
Mostly *kukui*
Shaded the route.
Through *puka* in the clouds -
I learned that word for hole today -
We could see the various changes
As we clip clopped along.
Perpendicular stone walls,
About 1,000 to 3,000 feet,
Guarded the valley
Like warriors of old.
The walls were plumed
With various bushes in places -
Forgive my lack of botanical terminology -
Swathed in waving ferns.

Transient pieces of clouds
Cast their shadows
Across the sunny bulwarks,
Mottling them with blots.
Billowy masses
Of fresh rainless, cotton clouds
Hid the summits.
If you've been to Europe,
The crater walls look like
The remains of old castles.
The highest peaks
Appeared and disappeared,
The fleeting clouds
like islands drifting in a fog.
Sometimes the cloudy curtain
Descended halfway down the valley,
Then shredded away
Leaving the canyon walls
Glorified in the sun again.
The valley was a mimic ruin
Of citadel ramparts and towers
Clothed in mosses
And garlands of swaying vines.
Suddenly, a verdure clad needle
Stepped out from around the corner.
I guess it was
A thousand feet high.
Some claim a literal translation, excrement;
an unfitting term for this obelisk.

The locals call it Pu`uokamoa
After a legend of a merman.
Gentlemen, some of you may have seen
The tourist stop down in Kealakekua,
The scraggly coconut stump that marks
Captain Cook's death,
The ruthless intrusion of Westerners.
Compared to the `Īao Needle,
As sailors call it,
There is no doubt as to
Which is the best monument.

REPORTER #1
When will you be leaving?

TWAIN
Sadly in a couple of days.
I've got to get back
To start work on a book.
I need the money to
Make these kinds of trips.

REPORTER #2
What are you calling it?

TWAIN
The book is called *Roughing It*.
It's in memory of your
Vulture sized mosquitos.

(Twain cont.)
Hey, enough talk.
Mrs. Texeira asked me to invite
You boys inside for some strong coffee
And…say, what do you call those
Little round Portuguese doughnuts?

REPORTER #1
Malasadas…

TWAIN
That's them, *Ono*, eh. Learned that
One too with all the delicious *kaukau*.
(The reporters and Twain gleefully enter
The hotel screen door.)

ʻĪAO THE NAVIGATOR
Twain's description of Maui,
Particularily that of ʻĪao
Would go around the world proclaiming
Its beauty with the appellation -
The Yosemite of the Pacific.
The serenity of the valley
Would be maintained for thirty years
Until a major catastrophe
Struck the valley.
It's Tuesday, January 18, 1916.
It had been pouring for hours.

(ʻĪao the Navigator cont.)
The *paniwai* or dam
Located up the valley
Was bulging at its seams.
With any further deluge of water
The dam could hold no more.
A few nervous hours later
The inevitable was realized.
The dam burst!
The surge sent a fifteen foot
Wall of water
Wiping out the kalo patches
And onto the sugar plantation village
Located in the flatlands.
Let's follow Deputy Sheriff Mahi.
He approaches
A classroom at Wailuku School
Where Sheriff Crowell has set up
A command post for relief efforts.

ACT SIX

OUTSIDE A CLASSROOM.
WAILUKU SCHOOL. 3 AM.

(Deputy Sheriff Mahi
Approaches the classroom.
He is in a raincoat and soaked.
He calls out to the sheriff.)

DEPUTY MAHI
Sheriff, you there?

SHERIFF CROWELL
Johnny, it's you!
So good to see you alive and well.
(Deputy takes off his raincoat.)
I've been worried about you.
Where's Junior?

DEPUTY MAHI
He's hanging out in
One of the evacuee classrooms.
The ladies are getting him
Some dry clothes
And some hot cocoa.
You know, Sheriff,
We were just a gallop away
From the rising on-rush.
We made it to the top of the hill
To see, sadly,
The Marquez house crash
Into Chung Qui's.
Sheriff, I can't believe it.
There were thirty homes
In the flat area;
Now they're gone.

SHERIFF CROWELL
I'm sorry to tell you,
Marquez never made it out.
Angus McPhee,
A couple of inmates, and I
Pulled his body
From lumber that had
Pinned him down in Happy Valley.
We spotted the body
When were trying to rescue some
Japanese ladies and a Filipino man
Who had found safety
In a huge monkey pod tree.

DEPUTY MAHI
You know, it's strange, Sheriff.
All night long
Junior Boy kept nagging me.
'I want to go to grandma's.'
'It's raining, Junior,' I told him.
'And I'm not
Taking you all the way to Pu`unene.
You have school tomorrow.'
He insisted,
'Something bad's going to happen.'
'It's just rain,' I told him.
'No, Daddy,' he moaned on.
'It's something bad.'
'Enough arguing,' I said.
'Now go to bed.'

He broke out in tears
and dragged his feet to bed.
I drowsed off
To the steady beat of the rain
On the tin roof.
Time passed.
Suddenly, I awoke to a crunching,
Tumbling chaos
As if Kamehameha's army was
Once again storming the valley.
It was a sound I had heard before -
With flash floods of a lesser scale.
A wall of water was headed
Our way.
I flung open Junior's bedroom door
Only to find his shivering little body
Already prepared to go.
His eyes were unslept,
His hands clutching
His scraggly teddy bear.
He had been drowsily standing there
Only waiting for my signal.
I grabbed him by the arm,
Raced him out of the house,
And tossed him onto Makua.
I jumped on, grabbed the reins
And kicked that old faithful like
He had never been kicked before;
Water splashing wildly as we
Galloped up the hill.

It was dark but I could still see
lumber, animals, and personal stuff
strewn across the valley floor.

SHERIFF CROWELL
And that's the problem right now,
Looters.
I've got to get back out there.
You get some food and coffee
And when you're ready,
Meet me in Happy Valley
To help search for the missing.
Joe Welch, Johnny Ho`opi`i
and David Kaina
Have been bringing people across
The stream since the deluge began.
They rigged up a block and tackle
That seems to be working well.
Gather up the volunteer deputies
Relieve them as needed.
I'll see you In a little while.
(He starts to leave.)

DEPUTY MAHI
Oh, Sheriff,
Do you have any idea of the losses?

SHERIFF CROWELL
On the desk…there's a copy.
I gotta go. (He exits.)

DEPUTY MAHI
(reading out loud)
Theodore Marquez - Filipino
Chung Qui - Chinese
Syetaki Jitsu - Japanese
Mrs. Cerilla Fernandez - Spanish
Infant Fernandez - 18 months
Juan Ramon Y Madronar - Spanish
Ramon Y Madronar
Mrs. Ramon Y Madronar
Infant Madronar - 2 months
Mrs. Sodetani - Japanese
Daughter of Mrs. Sodetani - 8 years
Infant Sodetani - 2 years.
…God…God bless their souls.
(The scene fades to black.)

`IAO THE NAVIGATOR
All bodies were eventually found
Minus the little Sodetani girl.
Come.
Follow me back where we started.
A river of delight,
A river of sacredness,
A river of tragedy.
The river and valley have had a full life
Similar to that of a human,
Filled with highs and lows.

(ʻĪao the Navigator cont.)
Liliʻuokalani,
Hawaii's last reigning monarch,
Would visit the valley
Several times before her death.
Her visit to ʻĪao
Seemed to be a renewed rallying
Cry for the reunification
Of the Hawaiian Kingdom.
She feasted and spoke
On the same hallowed
Ground of her ancestors,
Insensitively called -
The Dole Campgrounds.
After her visit,
A "mysterious" fire broke out,
Destroying the hales
That she had stayed in.
Today, some proclaim
What was uttered
Hundreds of years ago:
Nā e iki ʻĪao i ka uhiwai.
ʻĪao is barely breathing
in the heavy mist.'
It is a fragile valley;
It is a fragile river.
Embrace her past,
Preserve her future.
ʻ

(ʻĪao the Navigator cont.)
I must leave now
On my latest journey.
It's a journey
Into the hearts and minds
Of the lovers of Hawaiʻi
To stay the course
And protect the valley.
I go now, but you stay,
And finally enjoy,
From the eyes
Of those who have experienced -
ʻĪao Valley. (He exits. Fades to black)

(Music plays.
Slides of paintings,
sketches,
and photographs of ʻĪao Valley
and ʻĪao Stream are shown.
At the end, lights come up.

A PAU

GLOSSARY OF
WHERE WE WALK
THROUGH RAINBOWS

`Ae - yes
Awapuhi - forest
Ho`okele - to sail
Ino`a kapa kapa - nickname
Kahuna - specialist/ priest
Kapa - cloth made from mulberry bark
Kapu - forbidden
Koa - warrior
Kukui - oil from tree for lamp
Mahalo - thanks
Nā Makua - parents
Makuakāne - father
Makuahine - mother
Malo - loincloth
Manu - bird
Ma Uka (mauka) - toward the mountains
Moi - Chief/King
Mo`olelo - story
Oli - chant
Ono - delicious
`O`opu - fresh water fish
Paie`a - other name for Kamehameha I
Paniwai (Kepaniwai) - dam
Puka - hole

ISLAND SITES IN
WHERE WE WALK
THROUGH RAINBOWS

Happy Valley - village in Wailuku
`Iao - name of Jupiter
appearing as the morning star
Kahakuloa - land division West Maui
Kahului - area Central Maui
Kawelowelo - heiau near Wailuku
Mauna Kahālāwai - West Maui Mountains
Moloka`i - island at center of chain
O`ahu - northern island/ Honolulu capital
Olowalu - valley/village West Maui
Pāi`a - East Maui area
Pōhaku Ka`anapali - wharf West Maui
Pu`unene -area Central Maui
Waiehu - village oceanside of Wailuku
Waihe`e - North Maui village
Wailuku - Central Maui area/govt. seat

PŪNĀWAI PRESS

- e pua'i wale mai ana -

ABOUT THE AUTHOR

Born and raised on Maui, Wayne Moniz received a B.A. in English and Communications in 1968 from the University of Dayton, Ohio. In 1980 he was awarded an M.A. in Theater Arts - Film from UCLA. In 2005 he received the *Cades Award in Literature*, Hawaii's most prestigious writing prize for his body of work. His short story collection of Valley Isle tales won him the *Nā Palapala Po'okela* 2010 Readers' Choice Book of the Year. The audio book of *Under Maui Skies and Other Stories* was nominated for a Grammy in 2012 in the Spoken Word Category. Dubbed "The Dean of Maui Playwrights" by the *Maui News,* Wayne has written works that deal with the people, events, and issues of Hawai'i.

Pūnawai Press publishes dramas, screenplays, short stories, novels, poetry, non-fiction, and song lyrics about the people, events, and issues of Hawaìi.

To obtain more information, write to:
Pūnawai Press
1812 Nani St. • Wailuku, Maui • Hawaìì 96793

To purchase a copy of *Barefoot Boy in the Mango Tree:*
A Memoir of Maui and Me (autobiography)

Pūkoko: A Hawaiian in the American Civil War (novel)

Beyond the Reef: Stories of Maui in the World (short stories)

Ka Makani `Uhane -The Spirit Wind- (bio)

go online to AMAZON.COM

To purchase the book of
Under Maui Skies and Other Stories
Contact the author at
1812 Nani St.
Wailuku, Hawaìi 96793

To purchase
the Grammy nominated
audio book
Under Maui Skies and Other Stories
Go to undermauiskiesaudiobook.com
For more information about the book,
author, or artists, check them out on line.

Made in United States
Orlando, FL
05 January 2025

56560532R00146